D0732614

A NEW SONG FOR THE LORD

PREF
TRAN

Contents

The Cros
481 Eigh

Original
Liturgie i
Freiburg

English t
Company

All rights
in a retr
electronic
the writt

Printed i

Library

Ratzinge
[Ne
A n
Joseph
Marth

"A
Incl
ISB
1.
Liturg
BX19
264'.

3   4

Preface

❧

Throughout the years of the Liturgical Movement, as well as at the outset of the Second Vatican Council's reform of the liturgy, it appeared to many as if striving for the correct liturgical form were a purely pragmatic matter, a search for the form of worship most accessible to the people of our time. Since then it has become increasingly clear that liturgy involves our understanding of God and the world and our relationship to Christ, the Church, and ourselves. How we attend to liturgy determines the fate of the faith and the Church. For this reason liturgical matters have acquired an importance today that we were unable to envision before.

In the past decade I have been invited several times to give talks on liturgy and church music. Of course I was not able to comment on the issues involved from a musicological point of view, since I am by no means an authority on this subject; I could try to examine the complex of questions only from a theological perspective. Even when seen in this way, the topic seems to be rather distant from the center of our theological and liturgical inquiries and somewhat marginal. But the more I thought about it, the clearer it became that the nature of liturgy itself was at stake here. Thus, my contributions to liturgy and church music became all by themselves investigations into the nature of Christian worship. These studies, along with a paper on the Christian Sunday and a lecture on the significance of the house of God for the liturgy of Christians, constitute the main part of this book in which—I hope—perspectives on the essential elements of a theology of worship become accessible from different approaches.

Preceding the main section, part 2 of this book, are three papers on the Church's faith in Christ and on the hope of Christians that is grounded in him. Rereading these texts after an interval of several years, I became aware that our entire search for the criteria of liturgical renewal ultimately culminates in one question: Who do the people say that the Son of Man is? (Matt. 16:14f.). Hence, this first section seems to me to be imperative for placing liturgical questions in the right context. Only a close connection with Christology can make possible a productive development of the theology and practice of liturgy.

In a final section I have added an interview on Christian Penance and a paper on the path to the priesthood. When liturgy is understood correctly, it always reaches out beyond the Church into active life. This is most obvious in the case of Penance. The rite of Penance cannot simply be "celebrated"; penance must be lived and endured. But it needs liturgical support to give it direction and raise it from the level of mere morality with all its futilities into the realm of grace, into the sacrament. Over the last decades Penance has experienced a state of crisis like no other sacrament. Liturgy, however, is a whole made up of all the sacraments, and if an essential part of the whole becomes sick or almost becomes extinct, then the entire liturgy and all the other sacraments are at risk. For this reason it seems to me that a reflection on Penance as an integral whole composed of sacrament and life is imperative within the context of the liturgical question. I am well aware how inadequate my comments on Penance are. I nevertheless thought they should be included in this volume, at least for the sake of stimulating further reflection and research. Finally, the general question about our own preparation for worship seems to be reflected in a meaningful way in the question about the right way to prepare candidates for the priesthood; I therefore thought it fitting to include a meditation on this theme at the end of the book.

I have reworked all the articles for this collection in order to mold them into some sort of a whole. Nevertheless, repetitions could not be completely eliminated nor could the fragmentary nature of the individual contributions be overcome. In the end I can only hope that these endeavors with all their shortcomings can provide assistance to the faith and be of service to its realization in liturgy and life.

Joseph Cardinal Ratzinger
Rome, the Feast of the Transfiguration, 1994

Translator's Note

eͻ

Comments and clarifications in square brackets [ ] have been added by the translator. All the biblical quotations are from the *New Revised Standard Version* unless otherwise indicated. Greek words and phrases appear in transliteration.

Martha M. Matesich

PART
I

JESUS CHRIST, CENTER OF FAITH AND FOUNDATION OF OUR HOPE

☙

1

Jesus Christ Today

❧

COMMENTS ON THE ORIGIN AND PURPOSE OF THIS TEXT

I wrote the following essay in 1989 as the final lecture for a summer course at the Universidad Complutense in El Escorial near Madrid. For a week prior to this lecture theologians from different countries and denominations representing various theological disciplines had presented the participants with the whole range of current theological controversies surrounding the figure of Christ. At the close I was to offer a sort of synthesis of Christology for today.[1] I knew from the start that in the hour allotted to me I would be able only to suggest some contours and indicate a few directions. But which criteria was I to use for making this selection? To start with, it seemed advisable not to understand the "today" of the title too narrowly. Christ is first of all a historical figure; this means he has a "yesterday" that we cannot ignore. Thus, it was necessary to refer to the lasting significance of the historical dimension, about which others had already spoken in great detail. But Christ is risen and therefore is not locked into the past: we do encounter him today. Even the non-believer cannot deny that Christ appears today and that one would not ask about his past if it were not for this present. There is another factor, too: Jesus' whole message aims at leading people to the "kingdom of God." This means that the boundaries of time itself are transcended. I thought that in an introductory section I should talk about these dimensions of our belief in Christ and about some of the great images of Christ that have been developed in the course of history.

But which features of the image of Christ should be analyzed in the main part of the lecture? Again the word "today" provided the methodological key. At the time I was drafting the text, the considerable relevance of liberation theology was already on the wane, but those images and ideas of liberation theology that had outlived particular political settings came to light. First there was (and is) the notion of Christ the liberator, the leader in the new exodus from slavery to freedom. Next there is the "option for the poor": the poor Christ *is* God's option in person. Finally, in a world of violence, suffering, and death there is the cry for life, for him who can give life "in abundance." It seemed to me that the essence of the new experience of Christ in our time is expressed in these three closely connected approaches and for that reason a lecture that was to treat [the topic of] Christ today should include these images of hope for salvation as three modern titles for Christ, as it were.

If it were true, however, that the image of Christ today should be modeled on the actual Jesus of history, then I had to ask how these three images stood in relation to the biblical figure of Jesus. I could not strive for extensive scholarly analysis here; instead I had to seek an understanding that would make the connection between yesterday and today discernible in plain terms as well as point out, where necessary, the aspects of our present view that had to be corrected on the basis of scriptural witness. During the search for this understanding, my attention was drawn to a trilogy of titles in John's Gospel that in part resembles the modern triad in a striking way, although it cannot be made to correspond completely. In John's Gospel Jesus calls himself the way, the truth, and the life (John 14:6). Making the connection was easiest with the topic of life. Here one need ask only how our modern desire for life relates to the understanding of life that Jesus proclaims. What kind of life does he promise? How does it answer our questions? How can this life come to us?

Nor was it difficult to find a second connection: way and exodus have something to do with each other—exodus is the way from slavery to freedom. The five books of Moses show us this and the whole Old Testament is a meditation on this theme. In the Johannine concept of way, motifs in addition to exodus are operative, but this central idea of the Bible has without doubt also been adopted. Jesus calls himself the way, which entails a "theology of liberation." He then characterizes himself as the true Moses, who is more than the Moses of the Old Covenant—not just a leader on a way designated by God, but himself this very way. Hence, investigating the notion of way led to the New Testament core of liberation theology, helped to separate the true nature of this theology from false ideas, and consequently answered a basic question of our time (and of all human beings). Obviously, I was able only to allude to that in the lecture. The following was and is important to me: First of all, the question about Christ the liberator is a typical question of our times. Raising the question connects the historical figure of Christ to our present situation and assumes that there is a relationship between the current experience of being human and the biblical message. But the Bible itself, particularly in this case, has also been shaped by the connection between the Old Testament and the New Testament, that is, by two stages of the divine–human history of freedom. The essential mistake in the best known attempts at a liberation theology was reading this history backwards. This means that instead of progressing on the path of the history of liberation as the Bible describes it, from Moses to Christ and with Christ toward the kingdom of God, liberation theologians went in the opposite direction. They did not understand Moses in the movement toward Christ; instead, by subjecting Christ to political criteria they viewed the historical development the other way around. As a result, liberation theology also misunderstood Moses by omitting the dynamic that defines him and points forward. It is possible to err on the subject of exodus by forgetting the Old Testament; but one can also err by misjudging the uniqueness of the New Testament. In my attempt I was concerned about retaining the significance of the Old Testament without reduction, but also about understanding it as a path to the New Testament. I wanted to make comprehensible the new dimension of the concepts exodus, freedom, and liberation that came into the world through Christ.

Although it was not difficult to discover an inner relationship between the themes of way and liberation, and although the theme of life goes straight to the heart of our contemporary search, it seemed all the more impossible to establish a meaningful connection between the themes of truth and poverty. Making the trilogy "way, truth, life" correspond to the trilogy "freedom, poverty, life" appeared unfeasible at the middle point. The more I considered the matter, the clearer it became that precisely here a deep correlation is at work and that the theme of poverty reveals a new approach to the theme of truth. Historically, the theme of truth has been discredited by being connected with power. Christ rehabilitated truth for human beings by bringing it into the world devoid of all power, in the poverty of his mere preaching. In the third part of the lecture I attempted a closer examination of this correlation, which was at first unexpected and then came to the fore all the more meaningfully.

I refer here to two concrete statements of the lecture that are particularly important to me. First there is the theme of the imitation of Christ as a translation of the exodus motif into the practice of a lived life and as the possible and necessary exodus for everyone. The theme of following Christ suffers from a christological and anthropological error that is spreading. The opinion has become rather widespread that we can of course only imitate the human being Jesus, not the Son of God. Splitting Christ into a human model and a Son of God who does not concern us existentially diminishes and devalues the notion of imitation in such a way that returning to the larger dimension of the Old Testament becomes irresistible. In this respect one can very well understand the protest of liberation theology against the conventional Christian understanding of "way." No, by Christian exodus we mean the imitation of the whole and undivided Christ, that is, following his example into the divine as well. Only in this way does the theme of liberation acquire its proper dimension; anything else is kitschy and paltry. But how can this be done? How can human beings imitate the "Son" and follow the path "at the right hand of the Father"? Only with this quesion do we reach the pinnacle of the Christian theme of liberation. I have tried to answer it very briefly, but my response naturally needs further anthropological and theological elaboration.

I would like to ask the reader to pay special attention to yet a second statement that is connected to this. It concerns the question raised toward the end of the fourth section of whether monophysitism is a particular temptation in contemporary Christianity, especially in Western Christianity. Monophysitism, which attained its theoretical form in Egypt in the fifth century, refers to a narrowing of the image of Christ; this theory has threatened Christian consciousness time and again. The redeemer is denied a human nature of his own; human nature has been absorbed into divine nature and the two have become a single unity. Cutting short the human in Christ and seeing only the divine in him is a danger that can tempt the pious person in particular. During the religious awakening between the two World Wars a new sensitivity for the humanity of Jesus arose; one became aware of how pale the image of his humanity had become and how magnificently and intimately it speaks to us through the Gospels if we listen to them attentively. Above all, Karl Adam, at that time professor for dogmatics in Tübingen, knew how to speak to his contemporaries inspiringly about the man Jesus as he had encountered him in the Bible. While researching the history of liturgy, J. A. Jungmann reached the conclusion at about the same time that the suppression of Arianism, a theological movement that had denied the divinity of Christ, had led to a one-sided emphasis on the divinity of Jesus. It had given Christian prayer a kind of monophysitic momentum that had left a trail he tried relentlessly to expose in the analysis of the popular piety of his time.

Two different things relating to this question have to be clarified here. Unfortunately, the popular piety of the 1920s, to which both Karl Adam and Jungmann referred in their critical remarks, does not exist any more. For this reason their warnings cannot simply be applied to the present, totally apart from the question of whether their criticisms perhaps even then were not completely free of one-sided judgments. The other question is whether their historical analyses of the path from the New Testament to the early Church and from there to the Church of their time are accurate. Two contributions of these outstanding theologians to the question at hand do seem to me to be indisputable: (1) the new way of looking at the biblical figure of Jesus and at his humanity which touches us throughout the ages; (2) their emphatic reference to the christological synthesis of the Council of Chalcedon (A.D. 451), which defined once and for all the valid criterion for speaking correctly about Jesus Christ with its formula of the two natures in Christ held together by the one person of the Logos without division or separation.

Having said this, we now have to admit that ongoing research has also emphasized new aspects that force us to revise or at least to nuance some opinions. I do not wish to get involved in the dispute about the "historical Jesus" here, which has since become ever more muddled. There is, however, at least one thing that has become more and more clear: a reconstruction of the mere man Jesus separated from the mystery of his divine mission leads nowhere and invalidates itself. Prominent exegetes such as K. Berger and R. Pesch have shown us that only the biblical totality of the figure of Jesus makes sense. They have demonstrated that the ever more glaring illogic of those attempts to make Jesus fit into the reasonable human standards of his time necessitates a return to the indivisible figure of the Jesus of the Gospels. In terms of the history of liturgical prayer, modern research has shown that the anti-Arian rift is not as deep as Jungmann had supposed. According to his theory, people up to the fourth century did not pray to Jesus Christ but only to the Father. We can no longer adhere to this view today. From the beginning, invoking Jesus Christ has been part of the liturgy, without even taking into account the private praying of Christians.[2]

Above all else, however, the following is important: recent research has definitely not taken anything away from the greatness and normative function of the Council of Chalcedon, but it has made clear that the formula of Chalcedon was drawn up more out of a kind of intuition; only at subsequent councils was its meaning clarified, especially by the Third Council of Constantinople (680–681) and the Second Council of Nicea (787). Most of the time the christological models of the first half of our century went no further than Chalcedon, but Chalcedon is only completely understood when we read it in conjunction with the later councils. The theology of Maximus the Confessor (ca. 580–662) has proven increasingly to be indispensable for a proper understanding of faith in Christ as defined by the major councils. It was primarily Hans Urs von Balthasar who reintroduced Maximus's work into the theological debate;[3] then the research of M. J. Le Guillou, Chr. Schönborn, and others opened up further the understanding of this great witness from the close of the patristic age.[4] At the time when the humanity of Jesus was being newly emphasized, a few theologians went so far as to assert two different "I's" in Christ, a human one and a divine one.[5] In contrast, if one reads Maximus the Confessor and the later christological councils, one learns something different: Maximus emphatically warns us against a naturalistic idea of union as if God and the human in Christ were melted together into a hybrid being. The human and the divine remain two different natures, which also keep their distinctiveness in the God-man. Maximus warns us just as strongly against a dualistic conception, a kind of schizophrenia in which two persons would exist alongside each other. As a matter of fact, it did reach the point where Chalcedon's concept of person was relegated to the purely metaphysical realm and where the unity of the person was thereby negated in the concrete living of life. Maximus tells us no, there is no naturalistic fusion of the natures in Christ, but there is no schizophrenia in him either; rather there is the complete union on the personal level, the synthesis of freedoms from which a personal, not a natural, unity results. Concerning this point, the *Catechism of the Catholic Church* quotes the following words of Maximus: "The human nature of God's Son, *not by itself but by its union with the Word*, knew and showed forth in itself everything that pertains to God."[6] Why am I saying all of this? Because I think we are fighting windmills when we still rail against an assumed monophysitic danger today. In my opinion the danger in the 1930s was much less than the prominent theologians, brimming with enthusiasm for their new discoveries, thought at the time.[7] But that could be debated. Certainly there is no such danger as a significant movement in Christianity today. The threat for us is exactly the reverse—a one-sided separation Christology (Nestorianism) in which, when one reflects on the humanity of Christ, his divinity largely disappears, the unity of his person is dissolved, and reconstructions of merely the human Jesus dominate, which reflect more the ideas of our times than the true figure of our Lord. A main concern of the following section was and is to warn about the necessary change of the trend of our mainline theological positions.

PRELIMINARY REMARKS: TODAY, YESTERDAY, AND FOREVER

"Jesus Christ is the same yesterday and today and forever" (Heb. 13:8). This was the profession of those who had known Jesus on earth and had seen the Risen One. This means that we can see Jesus Christ correctly today only if we understand him in union with the Christ of "yesterday" and see in the Christ of yesterday and today the eternal Christ. The three dimensions of time as well as going beyond time into that which is simultaneously its origin and future are always a part of the encounter with Christ. If we are looking for the real Jesus, we must be prepared for this suspenseful tension. We usually encounter him in the present first: in the way he reveals himself now, in how people see and understand him, in how people live focused on him or against him, and in the way his words and deeds affect people today. But if this is not to remain simply second-hand knowledge, but is to become real knowledge, then we must go back and ask: Where does all this come from? Who was Jesus really at the time he lived as a man among other men and women?

We will have to listen to the sources which, by bearing witness to the origin, correct our present age when it gets lost in its own fantasies. This humble submission to the word of the sources, this willingness to let our dreams be snatched away from us and to obey reality is a basic condition for true encounter. Encounter demands the asceticism of truth, the humility of hearing and seeing which leads to the authentic grasping of the truth [*Wahr-Nehmen*].

Once again, however, there is a danger here that has gradually taken on truly dramatic forms as theology has progressed in the modern age. Modern theology begins in the

Enlightenment with the focus on the Christ of yesterday. Luther had already said that the Church had subordinated the Scriptures to itself and as a result had no longer listened to yesterday, to that historical "once" that cannot be repeated. Instead, the Church had only mirrored her own present and had thus disregarded the true Christ; the Church had proclaimed only a Christ today without his essential and fundamental yesterday; indeed, the Church had even made herself into Christ. The Enlightenment then treats this thought quite systematically and radically: Only the Christ of yesterday, the historical Christ, is in fact the real Christ; everything else is later fantasy. Christ *is* only what he *was*.[8] The search for the historical Jesus clearly locks Christ into the past. It denies him the today and the forever. Here I need not describe how the search for the Christ who really was slowly pushed both the Pauline and the Johannine Christ completely aside and finally also had to deny the Synoptic Jesus in order to fashion for itself, farther and farther behind all this, the Jesus who only was. But the more authentic this Jesus was supposed to be, the more fictitious he became through this rigid confinement to the past. Whoever wants to see Christ only yesterday does not find him; likewise, whoever would like to have him only today does not encounter him. Right from the beginning it is of his essence that he was, is, and will come again. Even as the living one, he has also always been the coming one. The message of his coming and staying belongs in a fundamental way to the image of himself. In turn, this claim to all the dimensions of time is based on his own understanding of his earthly life: he perceived it as a going forth from the Father and simultaneously as a remaining with him; thus he brought eternity into play with and connected it to time. If we deny ourselves an existence that can span these dimensions, we cannot comprehend him. One who understands time merely as a moment that irrevocably passes away and who lives accordingly thereby turns away in principle from what really makes up the figure of Jesus and what it seeks to convey. Knowledge is always a path. Those who reject the possibility of such an existence extended in time have in fact thereby denied themselves access to the sources that invite us to embark on this journey of being, which becomes a journey of discernment. Augustine once formulated these thoughts in an incomparably wonderful way:

> You, too, come to Christ. . . . Don't think of the long journeys. . . . One reaches him, the omnipresent one, through love, not by seafaring. Yet, since the floods and storms of manifold temptations are common enough on this voyage, too, believe in the crucified one so that your faith is capable of climbing onto the wood. Then you will not sink. . . .[9]

Let us summarize our thoughts up to this point: The first encounter with Jesus Christ occurs in the present; indeed, one can only encounter him because he is a today for many and therefore has a today. But to ensure that I get close to the whole Christ and not just to a piece of him perceived by chance, I must heed the Christ of yesterday as he reveals himself in the sources, especially in Scripture. If, in the process, I listen to him carefully and do not excise essential parts of his appearance because of a dogmatically asserted worldview, I see him open to the future and I see him coming from eternity, which embraces the past, the present, and the future, all at once. Where such a holistic understanding has been sought and lived, there Christ has always completely become "today," for only that which has roots in yesterday and powers of growth for tomorrow and which is in touch with the eternal beyond all time has real power over and in the present. The great periods in the history of faith have each produced its own image of Christ in this way; each period was capable of seeing him anew from the perspective of its own today and precisely in this way each period recognized "Christ yesterday and today and forever."

In early Christianity the "Christ of today" was seen primarily in the image of the shepherd who carries the lost sheep—humanity—on his shoulder.[10] Whoever looked at this image knew: I myself am this sheep. I had tried to get more of everything for my life; I had run after this or that dream until I had gotten caught in the pathless undergrowth and knew no way out. But he took me upon his shoulders and, carrying me, has himself become my way. In the next period there followed the image of the pantocrator. This soon turned into the attempt to portray the "historical Jesus" as he really was on earth, but it was accompanied by the conviction that God himself appears in the human being Jesus, that Jesus is God's icon and lets us see the invisible through the visible. As a consequence, looking at the picture becomes a way for humans to cross the boundary that would remain impassable for them without Christ. In the Romanesque period, the Latin Middle Ages represented the triumphant Christ on the cross and thus the cross as throne. Just as the icon of the Eastern Church seeks to show the invisible in the visible, so the Romanesque image of the cross would like to make the resurrection discernible in the Crucified One and thus make our own cross transparent to the promise that is concealed therein. In Gothic art the humanity of Jesus Christ becomes overwhelmingly evident: the cross is shown more and more in its pure, unmitigated horror, but the God who so namelessly suffers, who suffers as we do and more than we do without the light of the imminent triumph—precisely this God becomes the great comforter and the assurance of our salvation. Finally, in the image of the Pietà, Christ appears merely as a dead man on the lap of a mother who is left with nothing but sorrow: God seems to have died, to be dead in this world, and only the words from afar console: for the night sorrow, with the morning joy (cf. Ps. 30:5)—the knowledge that there is an Easter. The lesson of these images of "Christ today" remains valid because all of them are drawing on a vision that knows also Christ yesterday, tomorrow, and forever.[11]

I have spent so much time on these reflections because they provide the methodology for our topic. Drawing on the experiences and hardships of our times, contemporary theology has placed before us fascinating pictures of Christ today: Christ the liberator, the new Moses on the new exodus; Christ, the poor among the poor, as he shows himself in the beatitudes; Christ, the completely loving one whose being is both existence for others and existence for life itself [*Proexistenz*], and who expresses his deepest reality in the single word "for." Each of these images brings essential aspects of the figure of Jesus to light; each exposes us to fundamental questions: What is freedom, and where do we find the path that does not lead merely anywhere, but to real freedom, to the true "promised land" of human existence? What is the blessedness of poverty, and what must we do to attain this bliss for others and for ourselves? How do we deserve Christ's "being-for," and where does it lead us? Today there is fierce dispute on all these questions, which will always be productive if we do not seek to solve them solely from today's perspective, but also keep our view focused on the Christ of yesterday and in eternity. Within the limits of a lecture it is not possible to enter into this debate, which, although in the background, does state the central perspectives. Using the methodological starting point already proposed, I would like to select a different course, namely, to attach our current questioning and thinking to a biblical schema in order to pull it from there into the tension of yesterday—today—forever. I am thinking of the fundamental saying of the Johannine Christ: "I am the way, and the truth, and the life" (John 14:6). The idea of the *way* is related to the question of exodus in a manner that cannot be ignored. *Life* has become a key word of our times in the face of the threats of a "civilization" of death, which is in truth the loss of all civilization and culture; the motif of existence for others and for life itself [*Proexistenz*] involuntarily comes to mind here. *Truth*, however, is not one of the favorite notions of our times; truth is associated with intolerance and is judged to be a threat rather than a promise. But precisely for this reason it is important for us to ask about the truth and to let ourselves be asked about it from Christ's perspective.

CHRIST, THE WAY: EXODUS AND LIBERATION

Jesus Christ today—in our times we can see him first in the image of "way" as exodus, from the biblical perspective of the history of Israel: the way out into the open, into the wide open space of freedom. This expresses our awareness that we do not live in the open, that we are not where we actually belong. True, the new theology of exodus was first developed in connection with situations of political and economic oppression. It was concerned less with the form of government of this or that country than with the basic shape of our present world, which is built not on mutual solidarity but on a system of profit and hegemony that generates and also requires dependence. Strangely enough, people from the dominant nations are in no way happy with their type of freedom and power; they too feel that they are dependent on anonymous structures that take their breath away—and this even in those places where the form of government assures the greatest possible freedom. Paradoxically, the cry for liberation, for a new exodus into the land of true freedom sounds particularly loudly among those who have more possessions and mobility at their disposal than we could have ever imagined before. We are not where we should be, and we do not live as we would like to live. Where is the way? How can we traverse it? We find ourselves in the exact situation of the disciples to whom Jesus says: "And you know the way to the place where I am going," to which Thomas replies: "Lord, we do not know where you are going. How can we know the way?" (John 14:4–5).

There is only *one* place in the Gospels where the word "exodus" appears: in the Lukan account of the transfiguration. It says there that while Jesus was praying on the mountain his countenance changed and his raiment became dazzling white. Two men, Moses and Elijah, appeared in their glory and talked to him about the exodus he was about to accomplish in Jerusalem. Here the immediate sense of the word "exodus" is simply departure, death. Moses and Elijah, the two men who suffered greatly for the sake of God, are speaking of the passover of Jesus, the exodus of his cross. They are the two privileged witnesses of Jesus because they have preceded him along the way of passion. Both are valid interpreters of exodus: Moses, the leader of the exodus of Israel out of Egypt; and Elijah, who lived at a moment in the history of Israel when his people, although geographically in the promised land, had returned to Egypt in their mode of existence since they had forgotten God and were living under a tyrannical king through whom they had a tyrannical existence like the one they had experienced before the exodus. The message of Sinai, the covenantal instructions that were the inner goal of the exodus, had been thrown off as a fetter in order to achieve a self-made freedom, which proved to be the most extreme kind of tyranny. For this reason Elijah symbolically has to return to Sinai, has to retrace Israel's way in order to bring her anew the fruits of the exodus from God's mountain. The authentic nature of the exodus story thus becomes visible in Elijah: exodus refers neither to a geographical nor to a political way. This path cannot be traced on a geographical or political map. An exodus that does not lead to the covenant and does not find its "land" in living according to the covenant is not a true exodus.[12]

Two observations concerning the biblical text are important in this context. Whereas Luke begins his account with the more approximate time reference of "about eight days after these sayings," Matthew and Mark date the transfiguration exactly: six days after Peter's profession of faith and the subsequent promise of primacy. H. Gese has emphasized the Old Testament background of this time designation: "After six days of cloud-cover Moses climbed Mount Sinai and entered into the divine light" (see Exod. 24:16).[13] The high priest Aaron and the two priests Nadab and Abihu accompanied Moses here (Exod. 24:1), in much the same way as Peter, John, and James accompany Jesus. And just as Moses' face had become radiant through the encounter, so was Jesus transfigured in supernatural light. In the ancient event on Sinai God revealed himself in the formula with which he introduces himself, "I am YHWH," which is the start of the decalogue. Here we hear the call: "This is my Son, my Beloved; listen to him." Jesus is the living Torah, the covenant in person in whom the law turns to gift.

But Matthew's chronology contains yet a further dimension. J. M. van Cangh and M. van Esbroeck have uncovered the placement of the two events—Peter's profession of faith with the promise of primacy and the transfiguration—in the Jewish calendar of feasts and have thus revealed a more precise understanding of their significance. Accordingly, Peter's profession of faith occurs on Yom Kippur, the Day of Atonement; this is followed by five days of fasting and then by Sukkoth, the Feast of Booths, which resonates in the offer of three tents at the transfiguration.[14] Here we do not need to go into the whole spectrum of statements that results from this and concerns the two events as well as their inner connection. Let us emphasize what is essential for us: In the background there is, on the one hand, the mystery of atonement; on the other hand, the Feast of Booths, whose essence is simultaneously thanksgiving for the land and commemoration of the homelessness of the wayfarers. The exodus of Israel and the exodus of Jesus touch each other: all the feasts and all the ways of Israel lead to the passover of Jesus Christ.

Thus we can say: Jesus' "exit" in Jerusalem is the real and definitive exodus in which Christ walks the path into the open and himself becomes the way for humanity into the open, into freedom. In addition, if we include the fact that Luke depicts Jesus' entire public life as a going up to Jerusalem, then Jesus' whole existence appears as the exodus in which he is Moses as well as Israel. In order to understand all the dimensions of this way, however, we must also include the aspect of the resurrection. The Letter to the Hebrews describes the exodus of Jesus, whose road does not end in Jerusalem, from this perspective: He opened "the new and living way for us . . . through the curtain (that is, through his flesh)" (Heb. 10:20). His exodus leads beyond all that has been created into the "tent not made with hands," into contact with the living God (9:11). The promised land where he arrives and whither he leads is the state of being seated "at the right hand of God" (cf. Mark 12:36; Acts 2:33; Rom. 8:34, etc.). The thirst for freedom and liberation lives in every human being; but at every stage reached on this journey we become aware that it was only a stage and that nothing from what has been attained really corresponds to our desire. The thirst for freedom is the voice of our being made in the image and likeness of God; it is the thirst "to sit at the right hand of God," to be "like God." A liberator who wishes to deserve the name must push open the door to this reality, and all empirical forms of freedom have to measure up to it.

How does this happen? What does exodus really mean? The human person and humanity stood and stand before two paths here. There is the voice of the serpent, which says: "Step out of your self-incurred dependency; make yourself God and throw off the one who can never be anything but a limit for you." It is not surprising that some of the people who heard Christ's message identified him with the serpent and wanted to see him as the liberator from the old God.[15] But this is not his own way. What does it look like? There are two sayings of Jesus in which he relates the promise of sitting at the right hand to human beings. In the parable of the Last Judgment he speaks of the sheep which the king—the Son of Man—places on his right and to whom he gives the kingdom. They are the ones who gave him food when he was hungry, gave him drink when he was thirsty, welcomed him when he was a stranger and homeless, visited him when he was sick and in prison. They did this to him by doing it to the "least of these" in his family (Matt. 25:31–40). In the second text, the sons of Zebedee ask to be seated at the right and at the left of Jesus in his glory; they are told that sitting at the right or left depends on the will of the Father, but that it demands as its condition drinking the cup that Jesus drinks and receiving the baptism with which he is baptized (Mark 10:35–40).

We must bear both these comments in mind when we now return once again to the textual framework of Peter's profession of faith and the transfiguration, which belong together. The two events are connected to each other by the prophecy of death and resurrection, that is, by Jesus' own words about his exodus, which Peter, cherishing a completely different idea of exodus, opposes. For this Peter hears the retort: "Get behind me, Satan" (Matt. 16:23). Peter assumes the role of the devil the moment he disseminates the idea of an exodus without the cross—an exodus that leads not to the resurrection but to an earthly utopia. "Get behind me"—Jesus opposes this attempt to limit the exodus to an empirical goal with the command to follow him. The existential equivalent of the idea of the liberating way is following or imitation as the way into the open, as liberation.

Our understanding of the notion of following or imitation as the core of New Testament exodus theology must not, of course, be too narrow. The correct understanding of imitation depends on the correct understanding of the figure [*Gestalt*] of Jesus Christ. Imitation, following Jesus, should not be restricted to the moral dimension. It is a christological category, and only from there does it also become a moral task. Imitation, therefore, does not denote enough if one thinks of who Jesus is in terms that are too narrow. Whoever sees Jesus only as an advocate for a more open religion, for a more liberal morality, or for better political structures has to reduce imitation to the adoption of certain programmatic ideas. It then amounts to crediting Jesus with starting up a new platform, which others develop further; applying this platform can be interpreted as joining up with him. Such an imitation through having a platform in common is as arbitrary as it is inadequate, since the empirical conditions were very different then; whatever can supposedly be taken over from Jesus does not go beyond very general intentions. The recourse to such minimizations of the notion of imitation and hence of the message of exodus often rests on a logic that at first glance seems plausible: Jesus may have been both God and man, but *we* are, after all, only humans; *we* cannot imitate him in his divinity, but can follow him only as a human. With such an interpretation, however, we think all too little of human beings and of our own freedom and forsake the logic of the New Testament in which the bold sentence can be found: "Therefore be imitators of God" (Eph. 5:1).

No, the call to imitation is concerned not simply with a human agenda or with the human virtues of Jesus, but with his *entire* way, "through the curtain" (Heb. 10:20). What is essential and innovative about the way of Jesus Christ is exactly that he opens *this* way for us, for only in this manner do we come out into the open, into freedom. Imitation has the dimension of moving toward the divine communion, and this is why it is tied to the paschal mystery.[16] For this reason the saying of Jesus about following him that comes after Peter's profession of faith states: "If any want to become my followers, let them deny themselves and take up their cross and follow me" (Mark 8:34). This is not a narrow moralism that views life principally from the negative side, nor is it a kind of masochism for those who do not like themselves. We also do not track down the real meaning of Jesus' words if we understand them the other way around, as an exalted moralism for heroic souls who are determined to be martyrs. Jesus' call can only be comprehended from the broad paschal context of the entire exodus, which goes "through the curtain." From this goal the age-old wisdom of humans acquires its meaning—that only they who lose themselves find themselves, and only they who give life receive life (cf. Mark 8:35).

Imitation, therefore, is validly defined in those elements we found earlier in two of Jesus' sayings: baptism, cup, and love. The Church Fathers had the whole concept of imitation in full view. Rather than citing many texts, I would like to quote just one from St. Basil:

> The plan of God and our Redeemer for human beings consists in calling them back from exile and bringing them back from the alienation which came about because of disobedience. . . . For the perfection of life it is necessary to imitate Christ, not only in terms of the meekness, humility, and patience exhibited in his *life*, but also in terms of his *death*. . . . How do we achieve a similarity to his death? . . . What is to be won by this emulation? First of all, it is necessary to break through the form of our past life. According to the word of the Lord this is not possible if one is not reborn (cf. John 3:3). For rebirth is . . . the beginning of a second life. To begin a second life, however, one must put an end to the first. Just as for those who turn around on parallel tracks in a stadium there is a certain stopping and pause separating the movements in the opposite directions, so too, when lives change direction, there is obviously a death necessary between the lives which ends what has gone before and begins what is to follow."[17]

Now let us put this in plain terms: Christian exodus calls for a conversion which accepts the promise of Christ in its entirety and is prepared to lose its whole life to this promise. Conversion, then, also calls for going beyond self-reliance and for entrusting ourselves to the mystery, the sacrament in the community of the Church, in which God enters my life as agent and frees it from its isolation. Along with faith, conversion entails losing oneself in love, which is a resurrection since it is a kind of dying. Conversion is a cross held into the Easter mystery, although this does not mean it is less painful. After citing the words of the psalm "pierce my flesh with the nails of thy fear" (Ps. 119:120), Augustine expressed this in his inimitable way: "The nails are the commandments of justice: With these the fear of the Lord nails down the flesh [carnal desire] and crucifies us as a pleasing sacrifice unto himself."[18] In this way eternal life is always present in the midst of this life and exodus shines into a world that is in itself anything but a "promised land." In this manner Christ becomes the way—he himself, not just his words; and also in this way he becomes truly present "today."

CHRIST, THE TRUTH: TRUTH, FREEDOM, AND POVERTY

Let us now take at least a quick glance at the other two statements that belong together with "way": truth and life. Our age faces Christ's profession "I am the truth" with a skepticism similar to Pilate's—with the same arrogant yet resigned question: What is truth? Rather than in the words of Christ, people today recognize themselves in the fifth trope of Diogenes Laertius: "There is no truth. For some consider a thing just, others unjust, some good, others evil. Our motto, therefore, is: Reserve judgment on the truth."[19] Skepticism seems to be a dictate of tolerance and as such true wisdom. But we should not forget here that truth and freedom are inseparable. "I do not call you servants any longer," the Lord says, "because the servant does not know what the master is doing; but I have called you friends, because I have made known to you everything that I have heard from my Father" (John 15:15). Ignorance is dependency, slavery: whoever does not know remains a servant. Only when understanding opens up, when we begin to comprehend what is essential, do we begin to be free. Freedom from which truth has been removed is a lie. Christ the truth, this means: God who makes friends out of unknowing servants by letting us become, to some degree, sharers in the knowledge of himself. The image, friend of Christ, is dear to us, especially today, but his friendship consists in his having taken us into his trust, and the sphere of trust is truth.

When we speak today about knowledge as liberation from

the slavery of ignorance, we of course do not usually think of God, but of the "knowledge of control," knowledge about the technique for dealing with people and things. God remains on the sidelines; he does not seem important for the question about our ability to live. First we must know how to assert ourselves; once that is taken care of then we might leave room for contemplation too. In this restriction of the question of knowledge there lies not only the problem of our modern conception of truth and freedom but the very problem of our age in general. For it is assumed here that for shaping human matters and for forming our lives it is irrelevant whether there is a God or not. God seems to lie outside the functional contexts of our lives and of our society—the famous *Deus otiosus* of the history of religion.[20] But a God who is unimportant for human existence is not a God, for such a God lacks power and reality. If the world, however, does not come from a God and is not reigned over by him down to the smallest bit, then it does not come from freedom and consequently freedom has no power in it either; it is then a sum of compulsory mechanisms, and any freedom in it is merely pretense. Thus, coming from a different angle, we once again encounter the fact that freedom and truth are inseparable. If we can know nothing about God and if God does not want to know anything about us, then we are not free people in a creation that is open to freedom, but elements in a system of necessities in which, inexplicably, the cry for freedom will not die out. The question about God is simultaneously and in one the question about truth and freedom.

With that we have basically reached the point again where the paths of Arius and the official Church separate; it is the question about what is uniquely Christian and at the same time about the human capacity for truth. The real crux of Arius's heresy consists in his holding on to the idea of God's absolute transcendence which he had learned from the philosophy of late antiquity. This God cannot communicate himself; this God is too great and humans are too small; there is no contact between them. "The God of Arius stays locked into his impenetrable solitude; he is incapable of fully communicating his own life to the Son. Out of concern for God's transcendence Arius makes the one, supreme God a prisoner of his own greatness."[21] The world, therefore, is not God's creation either. This God cannot act outwardly; he is locked up in himself just as the world, consequently, is locked in itself. The world does not proclaim a creator, and God cannot make himself known. The human person does not become a "friend," for there is no bridge of trust. In a godless world we remain without truth and thus slaves.

A saying of the Johannine Christ is of great importance here: "Whoever has seen me has seen the Father" (John 14:9). Christoph Schönborn has shown impressively how the dispute about the icon of Christ reflects the deeper struggle surrounding the *capax dei* of human beings, that is, their capacity for truth and their call to freedom. What does a person who sees the man Jesus see? What can the icon that depicts the human Jesus show? According to some, one sees only the human being Jesus, nothing more, because God cannot be captured in pictures. God's divinity is in the "person" who as such cannot be "delineated" or made into an image. Exactly the opposite view has managed to assert itself as orthodox in the Church, that is, as the proper interpretation of Holy Scripture: Whoever sees Christ really sees the Father; in that which is visible one sees that which is invisible, the invisible in person. The visible form of Christ is not statically one-dimensional, nor to be understood as only belonging to the world of the senses, since the senses themselves are movements and starting points to things beyond themselves. They who look at the form of Christ are taken up into his exodus, which the Church Fathers explicitly mention in connection with the events on Mount Tabor. They are led on the paschal path of going beyond and learn to see more than just the visible in the visible.[22]

After major attempts by Athanasius and Gregory of Nyssa,

a first cognitive high point was reached in the work of Cyril of Alexandria. Cyril does not deny that the incarnation is, first of all, a disguising, a concealment of the glory of the Word. "The incomparable beauty of the divinity lets the humanity of Christ appear as nothing short of 'extreme ugliness.' Yet precisely this extreme degradation reveals the magnanimity of the love from which it arises. The sacrifice to the formlessness of death makes the love of the Father visible. . . . The crucified one is 'the image of the invisible God' (Col 1:15)."[23] The human life of Christ thus appears as "the image of the love of the Father made visible, the human translation of the eternal Sonship."[24] Maximus the Confessor brought this line of theological thought to its climax, creating a Christology that appears as one great interpretation of the words "Whoever sees me sees the Father." In the exodus of Christ's love—that is, in the transition from opposition to community which goes through the cross of obedience—redemption, that is, liberation, truly occurs. This exodus leads from the slavery of *philautia*, the slavery of self-conceit and self-containment, into the love of God: "In Christ, human nature has become capable of being like the love of God. . . . Love is God's icon."[25] For this reason, whoever sees Christ, the Crucified One, sees the Father—indeed, the entire trinitarian mystery. For we must add: If one sees the Father in Christ, then this means that in him the curtain of the temple is truly torn and the interior of God laid bare. For God, the one and only, is then revealed not as a monad but as Trinity. As a consequence, the human person has really become friend, initiated into the innermost mystery of God. This person is no longer a slave in a dark world, but knows the very heart of truth. But this truth is a way; it is the fatal, yet precisely through the losing of oneself life-giving adventure of love which alone is freedom.

During the period between the wars and in the decade before the Second Vatican Council, prominent theologians such as J. A. Jungmann, Karl Adam, Karl Rahner, and F. X.

Arnold talked about a factual monophysitism among pious people, about monophysitism as a danger in the Church of their times.[26] To what extent they judged the situation at that time correctly can remain an open question here, but it is evident that the danger today is exactly the opposite. It is not monophysitism that threatens Christianity but a new Arianism, or, to put it more mildly, at least a quite pronounced new Nestorianism to which, incidentally, with a kind of inner logic, a new iconoclasm corresponds. Maximus the Confessor is hardly a monophysite; he takes credit for essentially overcoming the last variety of monophysitism, namely, monothelitism. For him it is essential that precisely in Jesus, the human being, we are really looking at the Father; otherwise his whole theology of the Mount of Olives and the cross, of the exodus of humanity in the new Moses, would lose its meaning. But in the same way Maximus is also the most determined conqueror of Nestorianism, which cuts us off from the mystery of the Trinity and again makes the wall of transcendence essentially impassable. If we remain on this side of the wall, however, then we are slaves, not friends.[27]

I would still like to add a second comment. The idea of freedom and liberation automatically came to mind with the designation of Christ as "way." It now becomes clear that truth is also inseparably connected to freedom. In contrast to that, it seems farfetched if not even senseless to link the idea of the poor Christ to the theme of truth. And yet there is a profound connection here. Truth has been discredited in history by being presented in the pose of domination and being used as an excuse for violence and oppression. Plato already felt the danger that looms when people regard truth as a possession and therefore as a power making them superior. Being timid before the greatness of truth, he connected its affirmation with self-irony as an expression "of his own inadequacy, from which the highest degree of confidence, not skepticism," resulted.[28] In this manner the eighty-year-old Romano Guardini summarized Plato's understanding of truth and thereby described his own path, which had always been characterized both by a passionate affirmation of truth and by his own self-effacement. Plato's paradox between irony and truth seems to me to be an approach to the paradox of divine truth that shines forth precisely in the Crucified as extreme poverty and powerlessness: he is the icon of God because he is the manifestation of love, and for that reason the cross is his "glorification." In his treatise on love William of St. Thierry dramatically expressed the divine paradox that the truth of the trinitarian God, the highest glory, appears in the utmost poverty of the Crucified:

> When "the image of God," God the Son, saw how angels and human beings who had been made like God, i.e., in the image of God (without themselves being God's image) had perished through their disorderly grasping after the image. . . , he himself spoke: Woe be to you! Misery alone awakens no jealousy. . . . So I will offer myself to humans as the despised human and the least of all . . . so that they might burn with enthusiasm to imitate the humility in me; through this they should attain glory."[29]

The truth itself, the real truth, has become bearable for humans—indeed the way for them, by having appeared and appearing in the poverty of the powerless one. Not the rich glutton, but the despised Lazarus outside before the door represents the mystery of God the Son.[30] In Christ poverty has become the genuine sign, the inner "power" of truth. Only his true existence in poverty, nothing else, has opened the path for him into people's hearts. The humility of God is truth's door into the world; there is no other. Only in this manner can the truth become a way. What Paul said at the end of the Letter to the Galatians, after all the argumentation, endures: his last argument is comprised not of words but of the stigmata of Jesus which he carries on his body.[31] In the debate on true Christianity, on the right faith and the right way, the community of the cross is the final and decisive criterion.

CHRIST, THE LIFE:
EXISTENCE FOR OTHERS [*PROEXISTENZ*]

Our concluding consideration must take up at least briefly the third word in the self-proclamation of Jesus: Jesus the life. The fanatical greed for life encountered on every continent today has given rise to an anti-culture of death which is becoming the physiognomy of our times to an increasing degree. The unleashing of sexual desires, drugs, and the traffic in arms have become an unholy triad whose deadly net spans the continents ever more oppressively. Abortion, suicide, and collective violence are the concrete ways in which the syndicate of death operates; the immune deficiency AIDS has become a portrait of our culture's inner disease. There are no more factors of immunity for the soul. Positivistic intelligence does not offer the spiritual organism any ethical powers of immunity; it is rather the decay of the spiritual immune system and hence the helpless surrender to the mendacious promises of death which appear in the guise of more life. With the full force of its prowess, medical research is in the process of looking for vaccines against the disintegration of the body's power of immunity, and that is its duty. Nevertheless, it will only shift the area of destruction, not stop the victorious campaign of the anti-culture of death, if one does not realize at the same time that the bodily immune deficiency is an outcry of the misused creature, the human person. It is an image in which the real disease is represented: the helplessness of souls in a spiritual climate that declares null and void the real values of human life, God, and the soul.

If we Christians simply stand by and utter soothing words in this situation, we are completely superfluous. In order to meet the demands of the modern or postmodern age, it is not enough to submit ourselves to its standards and prove that we can keep up at the same time. This false kind of progressive Christianity would be merely ludicrous if it were not so sad and so dangerous. It accelerates the spiral of death instead of opposing it with the healing power of life. Marxist analysis, which some still want to use to show us the way out of the contradictions of our age, is an absurd anachronism in the face of the dominion of money and Cupid which represents the unifying bond in the satanic trinity of sex, drugs, and collective violence. If there is no fundamental healing of souls, these structural analyses are nothing but sheer superstition, which, by the way, only furthers the decomposition of the interior powers of immunity since it seeks to replace the powers of ethos with technology and mechanics—that is, with structures.

At this point the realism of Christianity must be rediscovered; Jesus Christ must be found in the present, and the meaning of the following words must be grasped anew: I am the way, the truth, and the life. A precise analysis of the illness would be necessary first, but that is not possible here. Let us content ourselves with the simple but basic question: Why do people take refuge in drugs? In general we can say that they do it because the life that presents itself to them is in reality too shallow, too deficient, too empty. After all the pleasures, all the emancipations, and all the hopes they have pinned to it, there remains a "much-too-little." To cope with life as trial and tribulation and to accept it at that become unbearable. Life should be a delight that gives of itself inexhaustibly and streams boundlessly. Two emotions are operative here: on the one hand, the greed for completeness, for infinity, which contrasts with the limitations of our life; on the other hand, the desire simply to have all this without pain, without effort. Life should give itself to humans without their giving themselves. We could therefore also say that the essence of the entire process is the denial of love, which leads to the flight into lies. But behind this is a false image of God, that is, the denial of God and the worship of an idol. Here one understands God as the rich man did, who could not hand over anything to Lazarus because he himself wanted to be a god; for this, however, the much he had was still too little. God is thus understood in the manner of Arius who thought that God cannot have any relationship outside of himself because only he is completely himself. Humans want to be such a god, one to whom everything flows and who gives nothing himself. This is why the true God is the real enemy, the competitor of those who have become inwardly blind in such a way. This is the real heart of their disease, for they then live a lie and are turned away from love, which is, also in the Trinity, an unconditional self-giving without limits. This being the case, the crucified Christ—Lazarus—is the true image of the trinitarian God. In him this trinitarian being—all the love and all the self-giving—becomes clearly visible.[32]

At this point we can perhaps begin to understand the meaning of a decisive saying from the priestly prayer of Jesus that at first sight might seem to be a completely unrealistic expression of a special religious world: "And this is eternal life, that they may know you, the only true God, and Jesus Christ whom you have sent" (John 17:3). Today we are generally no longer capable of seeing that the matter of God is something most real, indeed, the true key to our deepest human needs. This, however, shows how serious the sickness of our civilization is. Indeed, there will be no cure if God is not recognized as the structural core of our whole existence. Only in togetherness with God, being with God, does human life become real life. Without him it remains below its threshold and destroys itself. Redemptive togetherness or union with God, however, is possible only in the one whom he sent and through whom he himself is a God-with-us. We cannot "construct" this togetherness. Christ is the life because he leads us into this union with God. It is only from there that the wellspring of living water comes.

"Let anyone who is thirsty come to me," Christ says on the last, the most important day of the Festival of Booths (John 7:37). The feast commemorates Israel's thirst in the scorching heat of the waterless desert, which appears as a kingdom of death with no way out. Christ, however, proclaims himself to be the rock from which the inexhaustible fountain of fresh water gushes out: in death he becomes the fount of life.[33] Let anyone who is thirsty come: Has not the world with all its capabilities and power become a desert in which we can no longer find the living fount? Let anyone who is thirsty come: Even today he is the inexhaustible wellspring of living water. We need only come and drink so that the next sentence applies to us as well: "As the scripture has said, 'Out of the believer's heart shall flow rivers of living water'" (John 7:38). One cannot simply "take," simply receive, life—real life. It draws us into its dynamic of giving, into the dynamic of Christ who is life. To drink from the living water of the rock means to consent to the salvific mystery of water and blood. This is the radical antithesis of that greed which drives people to drugs. It is consenting to love; it is entering the truth. And exactly that is life.

NOTES

1. The lectures have been published in *Universidad Complutense de Madrid, Jesu Cristo hoy: Curses de Verano* (El Escorial, 1989).

2. See, e.g., B. Macomber, "The Ancient Form of the Anaphora of the Apostles," in *East of Byzantium*, ed. N. Garsoïan et al. (Washington, 1982), pp. 73–83, who proves that the invocation of Christ in the Anaphora of the Apostles from Addai and Mari is original and not a later addition. Note too A. Gerhards, "Prière adressée à Dieu ou au Christ?" in *Bibliotheca Eph. Lit., Subsidia* (Rome, 1983), pp. 101–14, which refers to other Anaphora from the period before the fourth century in which Christ was prayed to. "In contrast to Jungmann's view that it was not until the fourth century that prayers directed to Christ gradually found their way into the liturgy, praying to Christ was always a form that belonged to the public prayer of the Church" (p. 113). The cherubic hymn of the Byzantine liturgy is directed to Christ as the one who offers the sacrifice. The value of Jungmann's standard reference book, *Die Stellung Christi im liturgischen Gebet* [Eng.: *The Place of Christ in Liturgical Prayer* (New York, 1965)], has not been diminished by such isolated revisions. The work, first published in Münster, Ger-

many, in 1925, was reissued in 1962 with new supplements by the author.

3. H. U. von Balthasar, *Kosmische Liturgie: Das Weltbild Maximus' des Bekenners* (Freiburg, 1941; 2nd completely revised edition, Einsiedeln, 1961). See also W. Löser, *Im Geiste des Origenes: H. U. von Balthasar als Interpret der Theologie der Kirchenväter* (Frankfurt, 1976), pp. 181–212.

4. Chr. Schönborn, *Die Christus-Ikone: Eine theologische Hinführung* (Schaffhausen, 1984; originally French, Fribourg, 1976, 2nd ed. 1978), pp. 107–38; J.-M. Lethel, *Théologie de l'Agonie du Christ*, préface de M. J. Le Guillou (Paris, 1979).

5. See J. Ternus, "Das Seelen- und Bewusstseinsleben Jesu: Problemgeschichtlich-systematische Untersuchung," in *Das Konzil von Chalkedon: Geschichte und Gegenwart*, ed. A. Grillmeier and H. Bacht (Würzburg, 1954), pp. 81–237, especially pp. 136–42.

6. CCC 473.

7. It would be worthwhile today to discuss anew the questions that were highly stimulating at the time J. A. Jungmann raised them as well as to respond to new biases in the process; see Jungmann, *Die Frohbotschaft und unsere Glaubensverkündigung* (Regensburg, 1936) [Eng. abridged translation in *The Good News Yesterday and Today* (New York and Chicago, 1962)]. For example, his criticism of trinitarian piety (p. 70ff.), which he counters with a strictly christocentric position, should be reconsidered as well as his criticism of a piety toward Christ that is "monophysitically" colored. I would like to draw attention to just one passage in this criticism. On p. 77 the questionable nature of the sacramental hymn "Wir beten an dich, wahres Engelsbrot, Dich Vater, Herr, barmherzig grosser Gott" ["We pray to you, true bread of angels, you Father, Lord, mercifully great God"] is underscored. To address the Lord who is present in the Eucharist as "Father" is certainly not without its problems. All the same, applying the title of father to Christ reaches far back into the period before the Arian dispute; see R. Cantalamessa, "Il Cristo-Padre negli scritti del II–III secolo," *Rivista di Storia e Letteratura Religiosa* 3 (1967): 1–27; V. Grossi, "Il titolo cristologico 'Padre' nell'antichità cristiana," *Augustinianum* 16 (1976): 237–69; and B. Studer, *Gott und unsere Erlösung im Glauben der Alten Kirche* (Düsseldorf, 1985), p. 116. H. U. von Balthasar emphasized the spiritual significance and theological basis for such an address in a profound way in *Du hast Worte ewigen Lebens* (Einsiedeln and Trier, 1989), pp. 59–60. The erroneous and in no way justified translation of the end of the *Gloria*, where "in the glory of God the Father" (*in gloria Dei Patris*) has been distorted into a subordinationist-sounding "to the glory of God the Father," clearly shows how the dangers have been

reversed since Jungmann's critical comments. If one appeals to Phil. 2:11 for support (the text of the *Gloria* in its entire structure is completely independent of this), then it should be remembered that in New Testament Greek *en* and *eis* alternated and that the Old Latin versions as well as Jerome used the translation "in gloria Dei Patris" with good reason.

8. See H. Schlier's vivid analysis of the question: "Wer ist Jesus?" in *Der Geist und die Kirche: Exegetische Aufsätze und Vorträge*, ed. V. Kubina and K. Lehmann (Freiburg, 1980), pp. 20–32.

9. *Sermo* 131.2 (*PL* 38:730); German in H. U. von Balthasar, *Augustinus: Das Antlitz der Kirche* (Einsiedeln and Cologne, 1942), pp. 261–62 [translated into English from the German].

10. See F. van der Meer, *Christus: Der Menschensohn in der abendländischen Plastik* (Freiburg, 1980), p. 21; idem, *Die Ursprünge christlicher Kunst* (Freiburg, 1982), p. 88 and pp. 152ff. [Eng.: *Early Christian Art* (London, 1967)]; also instructive is F. Gerke, *Christus in der spätantiken Plastik*, 3rd ed. (Mainz, 1948).

2

Christ and the Church: Current Problems in Theology and Consequences for Catechesis

❦

To a large extent it is characteristic of the situation of faith and theology in Europe today that people are weary of the Church. The alternative "Jesus yes, the Church no" seems to be typical for the thinking of an entire generation. When confronted with this, our inclination to emphasize the positive aspects of the Church and her inseparability from Jesus is of little avail. We must dig deeper to understand the real difficulty our age has with faith. In the final analysis a christological problem lies behind the widespread notion that there is an antagonism between Jesus and the Church. The real antithesis we have to confront is not expressed in the formula "Jesus yes, the Church no"; instead it should be paraphrased with the words "Jesus yes, Christ no" or "Jesus yes, the Son of God no." We are experiencing a real Jesus-craze today that exhibits the greatest variety of features: Jesus in films, Jesus in rock operas, Jesus as catchword for critical-political options—all these phenomena express forms of religious enthusiasm or passion that would like to cling to the mysterious figure of Jesus and its inner strength, but at the same time do not want to know anything about what the faith of the Church and, grounding this, the faith of the evangelists say about Jesus. Jesus appears as one of the "authoritative human beings," as Karl Jaspers expressed it. His human side touches us; the profession that he is God's only-begotten Son merely seems to alienate him from us, to transpose him into the inaccessible, the unreal and to surrender him simultaneously to the management of ecclesiastical authority. Separating Jesus and Christ is at the same time separating Jesus and the Church: Christ is left to the Church since he seems to be her handiwork; in shoving Christ aside one hopes to win Jesus and with him a new form of freedom, of "redemption."

If the real crisis lies in Christology, not ecclesiology, then we must ask, Why? What are the roots of this split between Jesus and Christ, which, by the way, is already dealt with extensively in the First Letter of John? John, who treats the titles "Christ" and "Son of God" as equivalents (2:22 and 23; 4:15 and 5:1), repeatedly talks about people who say that Jesus is not the Christ (2:22; 4:3). He then calls those who deny that Jesus is the Christ antichrists. Perhaps this is actually the origin of the word "antichrist": to be against Jesus as the Christ, to deny him the predicate "Christ."

But let us ask about the roots of this contemporary attitude. There are of course many. One cause that is somewhat obvious but highly effective is the construction of a "historical Jesus" behind the Jesus of the Gospels. Using the criteria of the so-called modern worldview and the type of historiography inspired by the Enlightenment, one extracts Jesus from the sources and in opposition to the sources. In this process the following is assumed: Only that can happen in history which is in principle always possible; the normal causal framework is never interrupted, so that anything which goes against the causal laws known to us is not historical. Hence, the Jesus of the Gospels cannot be the real Jesus; a new one must be found, from whom everything is taken away that could be understandable only from God's perspective. The structural principle governing the making of this Jesus admits to excluding the divine in him: This historical Jesus can only be a non-Christ, a non-Son. Thus, it is no longer the Jesus of the Gospels speaking to those people today who rely on direction from this type of interpretation when reading the Bible, but the Jesus of the Enlightenment's philosophers, an "explained" Jesus. As a result, the Church falls apart all by herself; now she can only be an organization made by humans that tries, more or less skillfully and more or less benevolently, to put this Jesus to use. The sacraments, of course, fall by the wayside—how could there be a real presence of this "historical Jesus" in the Eucharist? What remains are symbols of community formation and rituals that hold the community together and stimulate it to take action in the world.

It has become clear that behind this reduction of Jesus which is represented in the catchword "historical Jesus" there lies a fundamental decision of an ideological nature that can be summed up in the slogan "modern worldview." We will have to come back to this later; first of all, however, we must examine a second point of departure that is causing the split between Jesus and Christ. If we have thus far spoken about a particular worldview, we must now consider a form of existential experience or, perhaps more accurately, a kind of experiential deficiency. Let us put it quite simply: People today no longer understand the Christian doctrine of redemption. It has no equivalent in their experience of life. Atonement, substitution, or satisfaction means nothing to them. What the word Christ or Messiah denoted is not part of their lives and thus remains an empty formula. In this way the profession that Jesus is Christ falls by the wayside all by itself. From here we can also explain the huge success of psychological interpretations of the Gospel, which now become the symbolic pre-realization of a redemptive curing of the spirit. For the same

reasons there has been wide acceptance of the political explanation of Christianity as presented to us in liberation theology,
which in the meantime has virtually failed. Redemption is
replaced by liberation in the modern sense, which can be
understood in a more psychological-individual or political-
collective way and which people like to connect with the myth
of progress. This Jesus *has* not redeemed us, but he can be a
role model for the way redemption or liberation comes about.
If, however, there is no already bestowed gift of redemption to
convey, but only instructions for our self-redemption, then the
Church as commonly understood is an absurdity, indeed an
outrage. She then has no authority in and of herself; under
these circumstances the authority she does claim is merely
assumed power. She should become a place of "freedom" in
the psychological or political sense instead. She should be the
place of our dreams of a liberated life. She cannot point to
anything transcendent, but must prove her worth as an inner-
worldly redemptive authority in every one of my own experiences. All that is unredeemed in my own existence and all that
displeases me about myself and others reflect on her.

In the end all this—the reduction of the world to what can
be proven and the reduction of our existence to what can be
experienced—is based on a third decisive process: the gradual
fading of the image of God which has steadily progressed
since the Enlightenment. Deism has virtually gained acceptance in the common consciousness. It is no longer possible to
imagine a God who takes care of the individual and really
acts in the world. If God exists at all, then maybe he initiated
the big bang, but nothing more than this remains for him in
the enlightened world. It seems almost ludicrous to think that
our good and bad deeds interest him, so small are we in contrast to the expanse of the universe. It also seems mythologi-
cal to ascribe activities in the world to him. There may indeed
be inexplicable occurrences, but we look for other causes for
them: superstition seems better grounded than faith; the
gods—that is, the unexplained powers we have to come to

terms with during the course of our lives—more believable than God. If in the end God has nothing to do with us, then the concept of sin also disappears. That a human deed could offend God has become a completely unthinkable thought for many. So there is really no further need for redemption in the classical sense of Christian faith since it hardly occurs to anyone to see sin as the cause of the misery in the world and in one's own life. Consequently there can naturally be no Son of God either who comes into the world to redeem us from sin and who for this dies on the cross. From here we can once again explain the fundamental change in the understanding of ritual and liturgy that has recently come about after a long time in the making: the primary subject of the liturgy is neither God nor Christ, but the "we" of the ones celebrating. And liturgy cannot of course have adoration as its primary content since, according to the deistic understanding of God, there is no reason for it. There is just as little reason for it to be concerned with atonement, sacrifice, or the forgiveness of sin. Instead, the point for those celebrating is to secure community with each other and thereby escape the isolation into which modern existence forces them. The point is to communicate experiences of liberation, joy, and reconciliation; denounce what is harmful; and provide impulses for action. For this reason the community has to create its own liturgy and not just receive it from traditions that have become unintelligible; it portrays itself and celebrates itself. Admittedly, we must not overlook a countermovement that is becoming ever more evident, particularly among the younger generation. To an increasing degree people are seeing through the banality and the childish rationalism of the pathetic homemade liturgies with their artificial theatrics; it is becoming obvious how trivial they are. The authority of mystery has disappeared, and the tiny self-affirmations with which one tries to make good this loss cannot even satisfy the functionaries in the long run, let alone those to whom such activities are supposed to appeal. Hence, the search for a true presence of redemption grows. Admittedly it does lead in very diverse directions. The huge rock festivals are occasions for letting existence run wild; they are raging antiliturgies where people are yanked out of themselves and where they can forget the dullness and commonness of everyday life. Drugs, too, belong to this category. On the other hand people are increasingly attracted to the magical and esoteric as the place where mystery supposedly reaches out to humans. Finally we can say that new places for faith emerge again where the liturgy is lit up by mystery.

Before we move on to the consequences of all this for catechesis, we must still consider a further important effect of the deistic worldview that continues to spread more or less consciously even among Christians today. Such an idea of God and of God's relation to humans affects moral theology in particular. It cannot be theology any longer but must become ethics, since God does not intervene in the world nor in the ways of people. What faith calls the commandments of God now appears as a cultural form of the historical behavior of humans. One can cite dependencies on and connections with other cultures, as well as developments and contradictions. All this seems sufficient to show that we are dealing only with rules of life formulated in individual societies. These depend on the assessment of human behavior and the goals of a culture; the more successfully these rules have been able to structure the cohesion of a society, secure its survival, and guarantee its cultural level, the more positively people rate them.

If one gets involved in such ideas and sees humanity as the only really acting subject of history, then other deficiencies of the modern worldview have a deep effect as well. From the perspective of belief in creation, the world had appeared as the crystallized idea of God. It carries a divine message in itself and as a result reveals valid norms for our behavior. But where God gives a push only to the beginning and then withdraws himself, things are no longer expressions of divine thinking and willing but merely products of evolution, that is, solely characterized by the law of survival and the struggle for self-preservation. From evolution we can then learn rules for asserting ourselves as a species. This, however, is something quite different from moral instruction in the sense of the old idea of "natural law." As the new demiurge, evolution does not recognize the category of the moral. Theology, of course, does not share such views, but neither has it sufficiently reflected on their significance. There remains in particular an uncertainty about God's action in history and about the connection between God and his creation that must necessarily have a negative effect on moral theology. For example, God's retreat from his world becomes clearly visible when one limits God to the transcendental sphere and says that he gives no "categorical" instructions. This results in God's becoming a general frame of reference without content; the meaning of moral conduct must then be determined solely within the world. The gradual disappearance of the concept of creation results in our not daring to think that God's great creational forms have an abiding nature; instead we limit nature to the purely empirical on the one hand and dissolve it into history on the other, which does not allow for permanent and public forms of virtuous activity. At the same time an extreme dualism between nature and history, between nature and human existence is exhibited here that can only be overcome by a renewal of belief in creation.

Let us not misunderstand each other. The person who in faith considers creation to be God's idea made flesh and who therefore finds moral direction in "nature" may on no account deny the significance of the historicity of human beings. We also have to admit that in the past there have been overextensions of "natural law," which does not simply present itself to us in the form of detailed instructions. Certainly it was not always sufficiently recognized that the nature of humans is connected to their historicity and shows itself at any one time in historical contexts. In this respect there is need for serious dialogue with the new views; the fact that "essence" (nature) and historicity coincide must be reconsidered. The huge amount of empirical knowledge that we have acquired through the natural and human sciences is of considerable importance for the moral issue: even someone who rejects a purely formal ethics and thinks that being itself is the source of moral norms cannot deny this. Conversely, however, we must not lose sight of what is permanent by looking at the historical development of what is human since we would then ultimately have to deny human beings themselves and break them up into a succession of states in which the typically human, the truly moral would also disappear. Moral theology thus faces great tasks, which can be dealt with properly only if it remains theology—that is, if God, the triune God revealed in Christ, is its foundation and center.

What follows from all this for catechesis? To begin with I must say that I can speak only about the contents here, not the methods, for which I am not responsible. But perhaps it is also useful to emphasize the priority of content over method which has been lost sight of in the past decades. Content determines method, not the other way around. From what has been discussed up to this point it also follows that we cannot assume there is a mutual understanding about Jesus Christ, that we have already agreed on this and only needed to try to make the Church more appealing as well. Confronted with the fact that many people today are deaf to divine matters, it is just as unthinkable for us to hide from the momentous questions of faith and escape into an anthropology or to try to justify the existence of the Church on the grounds of her social usefulness; as important as her social action is, it dies if the center of the Church, the mystery, vanishes. The focal points of today's catechesis which result from these considerations are, above all, the following:

1. Ultimately everything depends on the issue of God. Faith is belief in God or it does not exist. In the end it can be traced

back to this simple profession of belief in God, the living God from whom everything else comes. For this reason the question of God must be central in catechesis. The mystery of God, creator and redeemer, has to appear in all of its greatness. In addition we must put the myth of the modern worldview in its place. What is genuine science does not stand in the way of faith, but a lot of what only appears as science does. Even today, particularly today, belief in creation is reasonable; it must be the window to the majesty of God. This creation is not determined in such a way that only the mechanical has value in it or that love has no power in it. Because love is real and because it is power, God has power in the world. Or rather the other way around: Because God is the omnipotent one, it follows that love is power—the power we count on.

2. The form of Christ must be portrayed in all its dimensions. We should not be content with a fashionable Jesus; rather, it is from Jesus Christ that we discern God and from God that we discern Christ, and only in this do we see ourselves, do we find an answer to the question: How can we be human beings? Where is the key to ultimate happiness, to lasting happiness? Augustine was not afraid to go at the whole subject of Christianity from the perspective of thirst for happiness. If you get to the bottom of this thirst and do not stop at superficial things that quench it, you come to God, to Christ.

Just as we should not dodge the debate with modern myths concerning the problem of God, so too we can see the real Christ only if we unmask some of the pseudo-exegetical myths, if we see the authentic Jesus again in the Christ of the evangelists, the Christ of the witnesses who is truly historical in contrast to the artificial figure often presented under the label "historical Jesus." Here, too, we do not have to deny anything that is really scholarship; on the contrary, modern exegesis puts a wonderful treasure of new insights at our disposal wherever it is interpretation and not a hidden ideology.

The momentous moral questions of our age, which beset young people in particular, find their proper place only within the context of belief in God, the trinitarian God—Father, Son, and Holy Spirit—and only within the context of faith in the incarnate Son. Within this framework it will also become obvious that redemption is more than the fight for political utopias and more than psychotherapy. For we cannot shoulder the responsibility that the ethical challenges of our life impose on us if this responsibility is not supported by the redeeming love of God which comes toward us in the cross.

3. In order that such statements may become understandable and not remain simply foreign words from an unknown world, it is imperative to find a place to experience faith as the early Christian catechumenate did. Formerly the family and parish community provided this place of experience. The family generally does not serve this purpose any longer, and often the parish communities are not yet sufficiently prepared for their new responsibility which has arisen from the overall failure of the family as bearer of the faith tradition. The efficacy of the new evangelization depends on the success of once more establishing a community in which faith lives and in which its word can therefore be experienced as living, life-giving word.

3

God's Power—Our Hope

❧

The following contribution was given as a lecture to priests and pastoral assistants at the Court Church of Dresden on July 7, 1987, within the framework of the Dresden Catholic Conference (in the then GDR). It is concerned with the same struggle for a soteriological Christology which the two preceding texts also support, that is, the issue of how faith in Christ becomes redemption and salvation in our own lives.

LAYING THE FOUNDATIONS

Introductory Observations on the Essence of Power

There is something fascinating and simultaneously threatening about the word "power": all human beings dream of having power, of being able to manage things as they want, and in this way of being free and fearless in the world. But for most of us this remains a dream. We encounter power in the hands of others or—even worse—it confronts us as anonymous power since those who actually have it are not accessible. Power of this kind is experienced not as a hope but as a

45

nightmare and a threat. The fear that is circulating in our age in different guises is this fear of the anonymity of power which also denotes its uncontrollability: fear of the ecological threat to the roots of life caused by the unstoppable momentum of a technology that was created by humans as their power over nature but now threatens to become a force turned against them, a power that has slipped out of their control and dominates them rather than being the means by which they dominate. Besides that there is the fear of the danger arising from humanity's arsenals of weapons that were again created to demonstrate the power of one state over another but now seem to be expanding further with compulsive dynamism so that the question of whether they can be controlled by governments has become urgent. Even with the hopes for disarmament growing anew, we still fear the automated nature of this machinery and the danger of its setting itself off. Finally, there is the fear of the industrial and economic power structure as a whole, which threatens to reduce the individual to the submissiveness of a mere function.

Where then is God's power in the face of all these forms of power that threaten us? Does God have power in the world at all, in this world as it has become? Can his power be hope in the presence of these terrifying powers, or has God become sheer powerlessness? First it might be useful to call to mind at this point that humans once felt toward God's power the way we feel today toward the seemingly anonymous powers created by us. Because of the unpredictability of nature and fate, humans once saw themselves as at the mercy of an intangible, mysterious power that mostly seemed to be completely arbitrary. One either had to try to implore it on bended knee or keep it at bay by defending oneself. Magic is an attempt to procure a key to unknown forces and to penetrate their mystery so that we no longer confront them completely unarmed. It has been pointed out that technology translates this approach into the rational sphere with its attempt to grasp the functional structure of nature in order to be able to make it submissive. Of course this process presupposes the Christian demythologizing of the world, which assured humans that mysterious, divine powers do not threaten us. We live instead in a world created by God along rational lines, and he has entrusted this world to us so that we may rethink the thoughts of his reason with our reason and learn to govern, order, and shape the world according to his thoughts. As a consequence, however, God has appeared to be more and more superfluous and finally even burdensome and obstructive. Only the realm of subjectivity remained for God, since we now knew the objective side without him. In this sphere of subjectivity, however, God either becomes a mere feeling that counts for little or else appears as the listener eavesdropping at the door of my private life and spoiling my freedom. As insignificant as God has become, he is still the ultimate danger hampering my free self-development. Consequently, what magic had previously tried to do in nature begins again in a more subtle way: we must fend God off; he has to disappear; he must be uncovered in order to be opposed. Psycho analysis and psychotherapy are this magic of the inner self by which people assume power over their souls in order to be freed from the threat of God. But the soul we can see through is no longer free, and the power acquired over against God becomes a power of humans directed at themselves.

Is God's power then a threat or hope? Very few people still see it as a threat; God has moved too far away from us for that, and other threats have become too concrete instead. As to the other side of this question, even people of faith have more and more difficulty really seeing God as the hope of their lives and of our history and feeling secure in this hope. We must therefore now ask very concrete questions: Does God have power in the world? And, if so, what kind of power is it? Where and how does it manifest itself? How does it become accessible in concrete situations? What is its significance in our lives? What does it mean concretely for the priest and his co-workers here and now?

Two Biblical Texts on the Question of Power: The Mountain of Temptation and the Mountain of Mission

To answer the questions posed above I would like to begin with two texts from the Bible which represent in an antithetical way what God's power is not and what it is. At the same time these will shed light on the true essence of power and the true essence of hope. The first text is the account of the third temptation of Jesus (Matt. 4:8–10). Satan takes Jesus to a very high mountain and shows him all the kingdoms of the world and all their splendor. He claims to be the real ruler of the world who has power and delegates power. He offers Jesus power and its "splendor"—a word that will then reappear in the baptismal denunciation where in order to become a Christian one must renounce not only the devil but specifically his splendor. The splendor of power—this signifies being able to do what you want, enjoying what you want, having everything at your disposal and being able to choose the place of honor. No pleasure is turned down; every adventure is possible; everyone kneels before you. You may do everything you want and can do everything you want. It is that deceitful "being like God," that caricature of the likeness of God with which the devil always fools people and parodies God's freedom. Satan offers power—of course at his price: power based on terror, fear, selfishness, the rape of others, and the idolization of oneself. But—so he seems to be saying—that is exactly what power is. You cannot have it any other way. Whoever wants to dominate has to oppress, requires the threat of force, and should, on the other hand, get something out of it. And how should the world be redeemed if the redeemer does not have power? It is therefore perfectly obvious that the savior has to accept the offer of power and adhere to its methods if he wants to accomplish anything at all. This temptation has continued in this way throughout all of history. Over and again the powerful of the world have offered the Church power, and, along with this power, they have naturally tried to impose the methods of *their* power as well. But it is not the mission of the Church to set up a messianic kingdom in which human power poses and is worshiped as God's power. The power typical of political rule or technical management cannot be and must not be the style of the Church's power. By this statement we are not condemning civil power in general nor the sword which is subject to the criterion of justice as Rom. 13:1–7 shows. We are, however, condemning the identification of Church power with civil power and of God's power with civil power as well as the absolutizing of human power in general that this entails, as if this kind of power could itself be redemption. We are rejecting a particular concept of redemption, a false image of human beings and of God that makes a caricature of God by reducing the human being to the splendor of power and so to a pretense of humanity.

Let us interrupt our reflections for a moment to turn to the second text from Matthew's Gospel in which Jesus is again standing on a high mountain and the question of power comes up once more. It is the closing scene of the Gospel: the Risen One has called the eleven disciples to the mountain to commission them and pass on to them his promise for the future. He is again standing on the mountain, not by Satan's magic but through the power of God. He is again standing on the mountain and not only sees the kingdoms of the world with all their splendor but can now say: All power in heaven and on earth has been given to me. His power encompasses not only the earth but also heaven, and for this reason alone it is "all power." What he refused to take from the power of the devil is now really his, but in a completely different way, since it comes from a different source. He has become the Lord of heaven and earth who now sends his disciples forth as messengers and bearers of his power. But whence does this power come to him? And what sort of power is it?

First, let us point out that it is the Risen One who is speaking in this way. That is to say, he has passed through death, and only in this manner—through death, from the other side, and toward the other side—does he have power, which, however, for that very reason spans not only what appears, but everything—heaven and earth, and time up to its limits and beyond. To put it another way: Preceding this last appearance "on the mountain" there is another experience on a mountain that is located between these two accounts, separating them from each other and connecting them to each other. Jesus climbed the mountain of his crucifixion as Isaac had once climbed Moriah. Previously the devil had placed him on the pinnacle of the temple and on the top of the mountain, but now he is really "at the very top," raised "on high"; this "height," however, is the exact opposite of Satan's "heights." Satan's heights are the heights of doing things on one's own authority, of uninhibitedly determining oneself in possessing all things and being permitted all things. This nevertheless becomes a sham existence since the "all" that is possessed and enjoyed is always only a tiny bit, more of a nothing than a something, and the human person who has really been created for all things learns the futility of *this* "all" very well indeed. The height of the mountain of crucifixion consists in Jesus' having relinquished all possessions and privileges all the way down to the pure nothingness of complete nakedness, which then does not even have a place on the ground any more. He has put these things aside in his "thy will be done," which is spoken to the Father. He has put them aside in the complete unity of his will with the Father. In so doing he has attained the real "all"; he is at the highest peak of being—he is one with the true God, who is not a despot or pleasure-lover, but eternal truth and eternal love. The true image of God and of humans is thus restored in contrast to the caricature of God and humans which lay behind the satanic offer of "being like God." In his earthly nothingness but in unity with the will of God, Jesus also stood firm against the power of force and its being able to do all things. He is one with God and therefore one with the real power that encompasses heaven and earth, time and eternity. He is one with God, so that God's power has become his power. The power he now proclaims from the mountain of exaltation is power coming from the roots of the cross and is thus radically opposed to the unrestrained power of possessing all things, being allowed all things, and being able to do all things.

The Nature of Jesus' Power: Power in Obedience—Power Accepted as Responsibility

But we still have to ask more precisely: What exactly is the nature of this power? To what extent is it power at all? And what may we hope from it? Since all this is rather far away from our modern experiences of life, we must approach the reality of this power and our understanding of it gradually.

It seems to me that a linguistic observation is a helpful first step. To express this power of Jesus, the New Testament uses not a word that denotes the power inherent in a person, an existing concrete power, but the word *exousia*, which in Greek means the right to do something or a right over some-thing, a right that is itself grounded in the legal structure of a state. The word therefore describes a possibility of action officially given to a person as authority, right, permission, or freedom.[1] We are concerned here with a *conferred* power, which comes from a legal system, that is, from a form of jus-tice. Hence, it is authority derived from an underlying power, and for this reason it carries weight. It is power arising from obedience, a power grounded in an inner order for which one accepts the responsibility.

Thus, the word used in the Bible for Jesus' power already provides a profound interpretation of the essence of this power: it is not just the power of one's own physical or technical strength. It is not the power of an ancient or modern Goliath, but power stemming from obedience, that is, from a relationship that is responsibility for being, the responsibility of truth and the good. As portrayed in the hymn to Christ in Philippians (2:5–11), it is humble power. Christ does not hold on to equality with God as a thief holds on to his booty, as power captured at last that can be enjoyed to excess. The thief's way of thinking, which corresponds to the conventional idea of power, is in fact the very indication of powerlessness. What has been stolen does not really belong to him, and that is precisely why he greedily uses it and selfishly defends it. Romano Guardini has very beautifully described the positive content of the fundamental act of Jesus, his crucifixion and attendant exaltation, as it is portrayed in the hymn of Philippians: "Jesus' entire existence is the translation of power into humility . . . into obedience to the will of the Father. Obedience is not secondary for Jesus, but forms the core of his being. . . ."[2] For his power there is therefore "no limit coming from the outside, but only one from the inside . . . : the will of the Father freely accepted." It is a power that has such complete control over itself "that it is capable of renouncing itself."[3] We said: Jesus' power is power derived from obedience—the word itself already makes this clear. This means also that it is power that has the say in a legally structured system that as such is power. But this legally structured whole that stands behind and gives rise to Jesus' power is in the end not a sum of propositions but the will of God, the ordering of the good and the true, love in person. Thus, Jesus' power is power based on love, love becoming powerful. It is power that shows us the way from all that is tangible and visible to the invisible and the truly real of God's powerful love. It is power as way that has as its goal setting people on their way: into the transcendence of love. At this point we can briefly anticipate a third aspect that follows from this: Jesus has given his Church *exousia*. The Church participates in the authority of Jesus, and all power in her is nothing other than sharing in his authority and thus being placed under its measure and in its essential character.

Two Modes of Power:
The Power of Domination and the Power of Obedience

In summary we can say that God's power is explicitly revealed in the world in the power of Jesus Christ which comes from the unity of his will with the Father's and thus has its firmest foundation in the cross. Jesus' power has created a concrete place for itself in the world in the authority given to the Church. Before we extend this to the practical side of our lives as Church and as priests today, I would once more like to introduce a text from Scripture that illustrates the essence of false power in a fundamental way so that by testing the opposite position we see quite clearly what God's power means or does not mean in the world and for human beings. I am referring here to the account of the Fall (Genesis 3). Adam reaches for the fruit that promises to give him knowledge of good and evil. The crucial point here is that he is not interested in knowledge as knowledge, as perceiving the real in order to subject himself to it and live from this perception, that is, in accordance with it. The will formed in the conversation with the serpent is turned in just the opposite direction: Adam is looking for knowledge as power. He is not looking for knowledge to understand the language of being better or to listen more accurately and thus be able to obey more faithfully; instead he is seeking it because God's power has become suspicious and because he wants to counter it with equivalent power. He is seeking knowledge because he thinks that only in rebellion will humans be free. He himself wants to be a god, and by that he no longer understands having to listen, but only exercising power. Knowledge serves the purpose of taking hold, of dominating. It is purely functional, geared to use and domination. Such power does not entail responsibility, but is only being able and being in charge. Its nature appears to be nothing short of having no one over oneself and referring everything to oneself and one's own use so that power may become the "splendor of power."

Thus, the close connection between this scene and the three scriptural texts examined above—the mountain of Satan's promises, the mountain of the risen Crucified, and finally the reference to Adam as the counterimage to Jesus Christ in the Letter to the Philippians—becomes apparent. In the account of the Fall one sees what it looks like when one accepts Satan's offer of power. Power appears as the opposite of obedience and freedom as the opposite of responsibility; knowledge is separated from its ethical components and measured by the standard of conveying power. Without condemning science and technology, we still have to say that something of this fundamental attitude has found its way into the modern practice of seizing hold of nature.[4] A quotation from Thomas Hobbes is quite typical of this attitude: "Knowing a thing means knowing what you can do with it when you have it."[5] It should be clear that this does not represent the "dominion" over creation entrusted to humans by God (Gen. 1:28–30). Long before our ecological disputes, it was once again Romano Guardini who formulated very precisely what is meant by this right dominion: The human person "is lord by grace and should exercise dominion in responsibility toward him who is Lord by nature. . . . Dominion, therefore, does not mean that humans force their will upon what is given in nature but that they possess, shape, and create out of knowledge; this knowledge, however, accepts what each being is in and of itself."[6]

Let us now try to pull together what has been examined and ask once again: Does God have power in the world, and is this power hope for us? First of all we have to say: There is a type of power, the kind we are most familiar with, which opposes God and is interested only in not needing God any longer, indeed in eliminating him. The essence of such power consists in making mere objects and mere functions out of other things and other people and subjecting them to one's beck and call. Other things and other people are not looked upon as living realities in their own right to whose distinctiveness I must submit; they are dealt with as functions, that is, in the manner of a machine, as something dead. Hence, such power is ultimately the power of death, and it also inevitably pulls those who make use of it into the law of death and the dead. The law that such people force upon others becomes their own. Here God's word to Adam is really valid: If you eat of this fruit then you shall die (Gen. 2:17). It cannot be otherwise if power is understood as the opposite of obedience, for people are not the masters of being, even where they can dismantle it into large pieces and reassemble it like a machine. Notwithstanding, humans cannot live counter to being, and wherever they talk themselves into believing they can, they fall prey to the power of lies, that is, to the power of non-being, of the pretense of being and consequently to the power of death.

This power can of course be very tempting and make a strong impression. Its successes are only temporary, but this period can last a long time and dazzle someone who lives only for the moment. Yet this power is not the true and not the real power. The power that is found in being itself is stronger. Whoever is on its side has the upper hand. But the power of being is not one's own power; it is the power of the creator. In faith we know that the creator is not only truth but also love, and that the two cannot be separated. God has as much power in the world as truth and love. This would be a somewhat melancholy sentence if we were only to know that much of the world that we are able to grasp in the space of our own lives and experiences. But viewed from the new experience with God himself and with the world which God has given us in Jesus Christ, it is a sentence of triumphant hope. For now we can turn this sentence around: truth and love are identical with the power of God, since he not only has truth and love but is both of them. Thus, truth and love are the real, the ultimate power in the world. The hope of the Church is based on this, and the hope of Christians is based on this. Or, phrased better: For this reason Christian existence is hope. In this world much can be taken away from the Church, and she can suffer great and painful defeats. There is also much in the Church that repeatedly estranges her from what she really is, and this is constantly being taken out of her hands. She herself, however, does not go under. On the contrary, through all this what is truly hers only emerges anew and gathers new momentum. The vessel of the Church is the ship of hope. We can board it with confidence. The Lord of the world himself steers it and watches over it.

APPLICATIONS

In the first section of this article we have sought to understand what God's power is and why this power is not a threat, but hope for us. In a second set of reflections we now have to apply this to the life of the Church in general and to the life of priests and their co-workers in particular. We must ask: How can this power enter into our lives? How can it become hope for us and for all human beings at this moment in history? What is required in our situation for this hope to reach us and become our hope? Just as we did not discuss the fundamental questions of the first section on the essence of power in a systematically complete way, but more by way of examples and comments, so too we cannot be concerned— especially here—with developing a comprehensive theory of Christian life and priestly life regarding the power of God's hope. Without going into great systematic detail I would like to try simply to examine a few points that spring to mind automatically from what has already been considered.

Faith as the Door for God's Power

The fundamental insight discovered in the first section can be summarized in the statement: Power in the sense of the authority of Jesus Christ is power that arises from a relationship; it is power that is imparted in obedience and returns in responsibility. If this is true, then it follows that priests and correspondingly Christians in general must be people who live from and in a relationship—the relationship with God. The priest must be a believer, one who converses with God. If this is not the case, then all his activities are futile. The most lofty and important thing a priest can do for people is first of all being what he is: a believer. Through faith he lets God, the other, come into the world. And if the other is not at work, our work will never be enough. When people sense that one is there who believes, who lives with God and from God, hope becomes a reality for them as well. Through the faith of the priest, doors open up all around for the people: it is really possible to believe, even today. All human believing is a believing-with, and for this reason the one who believes before us is so important. In many ways this person is more exposed in his faith than the others, since their faith depends on his and since, at any given time, he has to withstand the hardships of faith for them. This is the reason why crises of the Church and of faith often make themselves felt sooner and more acutely among priests and religious than among the laity. There is also the danger that a priest takes the world of faith for granted or that it irritates him, that he becomes tired of it, first like the younger brother in the parable and then like the older. When this happens, people in the world, especially those who have found their way back to faith after experiencing the emptiness of the world, can do for him what the homecoming of the younger brother did for the older. They have experienced the deserts of the world and rediscovered the beauty of the house which has become a burden for the one who stayed. In this way there is a mutual give-and-take in faith in which priests and lay people become mediators of the nearness of God for one another. The priest must also nurture the humility of such receiving in himself. He must not allow that pride to awaken in him which we detect in the older brother: this good-for-nothing who is now enjoying home knows nothing about the burden of faithfulness. In our situation this pride often appears as a kind of arrogance that is typical of a specialist: What do these believing people in the world even know about the questions of biblical criticism and all the other kinds of criticism? What do they know about the misuse of power in the Church and about all the misery that is part of the Church's history? The arrogance of the specialist in matters of faith is a particularly intractable kind of blindness that is part of every know-it-all attitude. The faith that rediscovers the fresh water of God's word in the desert of a world emptied of God, at the pigs' trough of entertainment sprees gone hollow, such a faith may be inferior to the specialist in terms of knowledge about biblical text criticism, but for discerning the real that can be drawn from this well it is often infinitely superior to him. There will always be the fatigue of the older brother, but it should not lead to that intransigence which is no longer capable of hearing the wonderful words of the father: Everything I have is yours. The priest has to believe before others, but he also must be humble enough again and again to imitate and to cooperate with their faith. He strengthens their faith, but he also constantly receives faith from them.

By no means do we take it for granted when we say: We first let God's strength into the world by believing him. The first "task" a priest has to do is to be a believer and to become one ever anew and ever more. Faith is never simply there automatically; it must be lived. It leads us into conversation with God which involves speaking and listening to the same degree. Faith and prayer belong together; they cannot be separated. The time spent by a priest on prayer and listening to Scripture is never time lost to pastoral care or time withheld from others. People sense whether the work and words of their pastor spring from prayer or are fabricated at his desk. Above and beyond all activity, he must carry his congregation in prayer and into prayer and thus entrust it to God's power. Mutual give-and-take is certainly necessary here as well: praying always means praying with the whole praying Church, and hearing the Scriptures properly can take place only when listening with the Church.

Before we elaborate on these thoughts I would like to take up a further aspect of the theme of faith that emerges from the core of considerations made in the first section: faith is obedience. It is the unity of our will with God's will and precisely in this way imitation of Christ, for the essential aspect of his own path is his journey into unifying his will with God's will. The redemption of the world is founded on the prayer said on the Mount of Olives. not my will but thy will—on this prayer, which the Lord has handed over to us in the "Our Father" as the center of lived faith. But here we have at the same time also arrived at the Marian dimension of faith and of Christian existence. "Blessed are you who have believed" are Elizabeth's words of greeting to Mary. The act of faith by which she became God's door to the world and thus set free the place of hope, the "blessed" in her is by its very nature an act of obedience: Let it happen to me according to your will—with my very being I am in a relationship of service to you. Faith for her means making oneself available, saying yes. In an act of faith she offers God her own existence as a place for his work. Faith is not just one posture among others but directing your own being—toward the will of God and thus toward the will of truth and love. In his encyclical on Mary, the pope has interpreted her faith in a wonderfully profound way; what he says there should be an occasion for us to learn believing anew as the obedience of our entire existence through a contemplative understanding of and with Mary.[7] I would like to single out two elements from the encyclical that could lead to a more profound understanding of Mary's faith and thus of faith as obedience in general. First, there is the reference to Psalm 40:6–8, in which Hebrews (10:5–7) discovers the expression of that act of obedience of Jesus toward the Father which is accomplished in the incarnation and cross: "Sacrifice and offering you do not desire, but you have fashioned a body for me. . . . Behold I come . . . to do your will, O my God" [translation according to the somewhat different text of the ancient Greek version]. In Mary's yes to the birth of the Son of God from her womb through the power of the Holy Spirit, she makes her body, her whole self available as the place for God's action. In this word Mary's will and the will of the Son coincide. In the harmony of this yes, "a body you have prepared for me," the incarnation, the birth of God, becomes possible. For God's entry into this world, for God's birth to come about, there must be this Marian yes, this coincidence of our wills with his will over and over again.

This situation recurs in a new and definitive way on the cross. Nothing of the glory of the father David that had been mentioned in the words of prophecy is visible any more. Faith is hurtled into Abraham's situation, cast into utter darkness. "A body you have prepared for me, behold, I come"—this expression of readiness is now fully accepted, and precisely the darkness in which Mary stands is the completion of the communion of wills with him. Faith is the community of the cross, and only on the cross does it become complete. The place of final nondeliverance is the place where redemption really emerges. It seems to me that we have to relearn this piety of the cross in an entirely new way. It had appeared to us as too passive, too pessimistic, sentimental—but if we do not practice the cross, how will we be able to carry it when it is imposed upon us? A friend of mine who was dependent on kidney dialysis for years and had to experience how his life was gradually slipping away from him once told me that as a child he especially loved the stations of the cross and liked to do them later in life as well. When he learned of the awful diagnosis, he was at first stunned, but then it suddenly occurred to him: What you have always prayed is now becoming serious; now you may really accompany him and be taken up into the way of the cross by him. In this way my friend regained his serenity, which radiated from him right up to the end and let the brilliance of faith shine forth for all to see. To express it with Guardini's words: We have to relearn "what kind of liberating power lies in overcoming oneself; how suffering which is inwardly accepted transforms a person; and how all essential growth not only depends on work, but also on freely offered sacrifice."[8]

Scripture as the Place of God's Hope-Instilling Power

Faith is obedience; it means that we relearn the essential form of our being—our nature as creatures—and in this way become authentic [*wahr werden*]. It means that we recognize the relationship of responsibility as the basic form of our lives and that as a result power changes from being a threat and a danger to hope. This obedience is directed to God himself— on the one hand it presupposes an attentive and vital relationship with God, and on the other hand it makes this possible, for only the obedient person perceives God. To ensure, however, that our obedience becomes concrete and is not inadvertently equated with the projections of our own desires, God has made himself concrete in many different ways—to begin with, in his words. Thus, obedience to God is a relationship of obedience to his word. We have to enter into a relationship of awe and obedience toward the Bible, which nowadays is frequently in danger of being lost. If individuals or different groups continually create their own Bible by means of separating the sources and criticizing the tradition and then place this Bible in opposition to the unity of Scripture and the Church, this is no longer obedience to God's word. It is rather an apotheosis of their own position with the help of a text-montage whose selection and omissions are ultimately based on the positions they want. Historical-critical exegesis can be a wonderful means for a deeper understanding of the Bible if its instruments are used with that reverent love which seeks to know God's gift in the most exact and careful way possible. It does not, however, achieve its purpose when it is no longer a path to more careful listening but keeps the text on tenterhooks, so to speak, in order to coerce answers from it which it wanted to withhold. In the fourth century Gregory of Nyssa already dealt with these questions in a way that is still valid in his debate with the theological rationalist Eunomius. Eunomius had maintained that it was possible to form a completely satisfactory concept of God which really grasped and accurately described God's being. Gregory responded that Eunomius had tried "to encompass the unfathomable nature of God in the span of a child's hand." Scientific thinking naturally aims at this kind of comprehension; it tries to take things in hand so that we can have them at hand. "It transforms each mystery into a 'thing.' Gregory calls this *physiologein*, i.e., 'to treat in a scientific way.' But the mystery of theology is one thing and the science about natures something else."[9]

Is there not too much *physiologein* in our exegesis and our modern way of dealing with Scripture? Are we not in fact treating it as we treat matter in the laboratory? Do we not indeed turn it into a dead thing that we assemble and disassemble at our pleasure? And where in this process is the essence of interpretation which not only views the words as a dead collection of texts but hears the living Speaker himself in them? If even human speech boundlessly transcends itself the greater it is and refers to the unsaid and inexhaustible beyond the words themselves, how much more must this be true of the word whose ultimate and real subject we believe to be God himself? Must we not once again develop methods that respect this inner self-transcending of the words into the word of God, methods that are open to grasping the experiences of the saints with this word—those people who not only read the word but lived it to the full?

I would like to return to Gregory of Nyssa once again, in whose work I found a metaphor for the right way to treat Scripture, which can at first cause us to smile because of its allegorical point of departure, but which then—viewed in its real profundity—has a great deal to say to us. The metaphor is found in his interpretation of the laws for the Jewish Passover meal. Gregory starts from the assumption that the word of God is our food, and from there he takes the liberty of applying the laws for the meal to the way we treat the Bible as well. Two of the ordinances seem to him to be particularly worthy of reflection: The food must be eaten fresh from the fire; and one is not allowed to break the bones. Fire is a metaphor for the Holy Spirit: Does not this ordinance mean that we are not permitted to take the food away from the sphere of the living fire, that we are not permitted to let it get cold? Does it not mean that reading Scriptures must occur in the fire, that is, in the community of the Holy Spirit, in the living faith that connects us with the origin of the food? On the other hand—there are bones we cannot grasp—the overwhelming questions that force themselves upon us and with which we cannot cope. "What is the essence of God? What was there before creation? What lies beyond the visible world? What kind of necessity underlies everything that happens?" Today we would add a lot of further questions which distress us even more. "Do not break the bones"—this means: "To know all this is only befitting of the Holy Spirit. . . ." "Do not break the bones"—Gregory now interprets this verse with a saying from the Book of Wisdom: "Do not meddle in matters that are beyond you" (Sir. 3:23).[10] He could also have referred to Paul, who warns "not to think of yourself more highly than you ought to think, but to think with sober judgment, each according to the measure of faith that God has assigned" (Rom. 12:3: *hyperphronein—phronein—sophronein*).[11] Are we not frequently breaking the bones of Scripture today by breaking it open much further than the measure given to us? And do we not often receive its words as cold, indigestible food very far away from the fire of the Holy Spirit, the fire of living faith?

If we dwell on Paul's words in the Letter to the Romans for a moment longer, another side of all this is revealed. For the apostle, practicing moderation in one's own way of reflecting on divine mystery is above all else also fitting oneself into the measure of faith of the body of Christ, the Church.[12] Today even Catholics frequently use Scripture as a weapon against the Church. As the Word of God, it certainly does stand above the Church, which must constantly let herself be judged and purified by it. But it does not stand apart from the body of Christ—a privatized reading can never penetrate the core of Scripture. Proper reading of Scripture presupposes that we read it where it has made and still makes history, where it is not witness to the past but the vital strength of the present: in the Church of the Lord and with her eyes, the eyes of faith. In this sense obedience to Scripture is always obedience to the Church; this obedience becomes abstract if we try to remove the Church from the Bible or even try to play her off against it. Scripture alive in the living Church is also God's present power in the world today—a power which remains an inexhaustible source of hope throughout all generations.

The Authority of the Church and the Power of God

We have now arrived at a further aspect of the topic of obedience: obedience toward the Church. We find this particularly difficult to accept today. At the outset we stated that the sinister feature about those who presently hold power, the large state and economic institutions, is their anonymity and inaccessibility. We are afraid of the powerful government and economic bodies and mighty political parties looming before us like gigantic polyps that inevitably grasp the individual. In people's perception today the large, organized churches also appear as such instruments of anonymous power and thus not as a hope, but as a danger. It is felt that these churches are part of the establishment and collaborators in the conspiracy of power. Confronted with the increasing anonymity and uniformity of the world, people seek refuge in small groups, whether they are called "base communities," "the Church from below," or whatever. Here they experience sympathy and good will; here mutual understanding rules, not laws. A little oasis of humanness in the spirit of Jesus seems to open up, but unfortunately it is constantly being disrupted by the unreasonable demands and manifestations of the larger Church, which exercises her power and, with her ancient ideas, mercilessly rides roughshod over the group's beautiful world. The result is group against Church, parish community against institution. Where the community represents the place for hope, the institution stands for the threat of the powerful. Two things are correct here.

The Church needs the environment of life in miniature where faith is concretized and becomes an oasis of humanness. The forms change: the Middle Ages were familiar with the confraternities and the Third Orders; the baroque period brought both back to life; and today other names and forms may surface instead. Now and then such communal formation can be burdened with conflicts, but it has always been welcomed by the official Church and is unquestionably supported by the new canon law. It is also correct that in the past two decades an excessive amount of institutionalization has come about in the Church, which is alarming. The wish to participate, which is in and of itself justified, has produced ever new organizational bodies, so that those people who simply try to live unpretentiously as Christians in their Church and who would like to find nothing else in her except the communion of Word and sacrament are beginning to feel disqualified. In this situation a church in the diaspora is probably more fortunate because it does not have as many possibilities for the ostentation we observe everywhere in the Western world. Here we are confronted with a tangle of authorities which almost inevitably triggers feelings of their inscrutability and our powerlessness and which can also easily obstruct the view of what is really important. Future reforms should therefore aim not at the creation of yet more institutions, but at their reduction.

Having said this, I must, however, also criticize what is fundamentally wrong in remarks I frequently hear from basically hard-working and good priests who say, "Well, the way Christianity is presented in our parish it would appeal to youth, but then the impression made by the official Church ruins everything for us again." I do not want to waste time on the absurdity of the expression "official Church"; the more dangerous nonsense lies in the confrontation depicted here. That a youth group likes the assistant pastor better than the bishop is nothing out of the ordinary. But that this results in a confrontation between two ideas of church is no longer normal. For if the assent to Christianity is no longer addressed to the whole of the Church, but only to its amiable representation in the person of the priest or lay leader, then such an assent is certainly built on sand—on someone speaking in his or her own name. The motivator's personal ability now counts more than the authority in which he or she stands. As a result, however—even if at first no one is conscious of it at all—authority is being replaced with power, power that has been given and must be returned through one's own ability. The structure of *exousia* about which we spoke in the first part has been abandoned, and as a consequence what is essential has been lost. What makes the Church real is not that there are likable people in her, which is really always desirable and will certainly always be the case as well. The reality is her *exousia*: she is given the power, the authority to speak words of salvation and to perform deeds of salvation which humans need and can never achieve on their own. No one can usurp the "I" of Christ or the "I" of God. The priest speaks with this "I" when he says: "This is my body" and when he says "I forgive you your sins." It is not the priest who forgives them—that would not count for much—but God who forgives them, and this definitely changes everything. But what a shaking event it is that a human being is permitted to utter the "I" of God! The priest can do it only on the basis of that authority which the Lord has given his Church. Without this authority he is nothing but a social worker. That is an honorable profession, but in the Church we are looking for higher hopes, which come from a greater power. If these words of authority are no longer spoken and if they no longer remain transparent so that their foundation is visible, then the human warmth of the small group is of little use. What is essential has been lost, and the group will become aware of this very soon. It must not be spared the pain of conversion, which expects of us what we cannot achieve on our own and leads us precisely in this way into that sphere of God's power which is our true hope.

The authority of the Church is transparent to God's power and consequently our hope. For this reason the inner commitment to the authority of the Church in an act of profound obedience is the fundamental decision of priestly existence. A community that does not like itself cannot endure, and an officeholder who turns against the inner locus of his ministry can neither serve others nor lead a fulfilled life. As we have already mentioned, there are various reasons why the reality "Church," which seemed to experience an awakening in souls in such a promising way during the 1920s, appears as a foreign, alienating, mega-institution today. But one crucial cause comes to light especially when the officeholder who should personalize the institution and make it present in his person becomes a wall instead of a window, opposes it instead of letting it become, in the suffering and struggle of his own faith, something close to us worthy of trust. This extreme case of opposition is certainly not very frequent in its crassest form—thank God. The Church is alive not least of all because there are so many good priests, expecially today, who embody it as a place of hope. But temptations also exist, and with inner alertness and readiness each of us must struggle ever anew not to be pushed in the wrong direction.

The theme of obedience has grown far beyond what I initially intended to say. I actually also wanted to discuss a number of other attitudes in which God's power is present as hope in the Church: asceticism, humility, penance; the natural and the supernatural virtues; also the great basic ministries, *martyria, diakonia,* and *leitourgia.* And above all: love and its concrete forms in parish life. All that is not possible any more; somehow—I hope—the starting points for all these are included in what I have described. In the end I have been concerned about explaining what love is all along. For the essence of God's power is love, and that is why it is hope for all of us. It can happen again and again that a priest and then the Church stand in the way of this power and this hope. That is the sin we confess, and we must ask the Lord to prevail over it. But God is the stronger one. He does not withdraw his authority from the Church, and this authority which comes toward us in Word and sacrament is, also today, a light illuminating us—hope that bestows life and a future.

NOTES

1. See W. Foerster, *"exousia,"* *Theological Dictionary of the New Testament,* trans. and ed. G. W. Bromiley (Grand Rapids, Mich.: Eerdmans, 1964–74) 2:562–75, especially pp. 562–63 and p. 566.

2. R. Guardini, *Die Macht: Versuch einer Wegweisung* (Würzburg, 1952), p. 38.

3. Ibid., p. 39.

4. For important reflections on this topic, see C. S. Lewis, *Die Abschaffung des Menschen* (Einsiedeln, 1979), especially pp. 72ff. [Eng.: *The Abolition of Man or Reflections on Education with Special Reference to the Teaching of English in the Upper Forms of Schools,* 14th pr. (New York: Macmillan, 1976)].

5. Quoted in R. Spaemann, *Die Unantastbarkeit des menschlichen Lebens: Kommentar zur Instruktion der Kongregation für die*

Glaubenslehre über ethische Fragen der Biomedizin (Freiburg, 1987), p. 71.

6. R. Guardini, *Die Macht* (see n. 2), pp. 26–27.

7. Here I am discussing ideas that I have developed more thoroughly in my guide to the encyclical published by Herder: *Maria—Gottes Ja zum Menschen: Papst Johannes Paul II., Enzyklika "Mutter des Erlösers"* (Freiburg, 1987), pp. 116ff.

8. R. Guardini, *Die Macht* (see n. 2), p. 99. T. Goritschewa strikingly emphasizes the correlation between suffering and grace and suffering and redemption in her book *Die Kraft der Ohnmächtigen: Weisheit aus dem Leiden* (Wuppertal, 1987), see especially pp. 21–25.

9. H. U. von Balthasar in his introduction to *Gregor von Nyssa, Der versiegelte Quell: Auslegung des Hohen Liedes*, 3rd ed. (Einsiedeln, 1984), p. 17.

10. Gregory of Nyssa, "De vita Moysis," *PG* 44:357 B–D; German translation: *Der Aufstieg des Moses*, trans. and introduced by M. Blum (Freiburg, 1963), pp. 76–77. [The passages quoted in the text have been translated into English from the German.]

11. See H. Schlier, *Der Römerbrief* (Freiburg, 1977), pp. 363–69.

12. Ibid., p. 368: "*Hyperphronein* evidently consists in the effort of one member of the community, regardless of his or her own measure of faith, to match or even be superior to the others. *Sophronein*, however, is the particular endeavor to safeguard and foster the unity of the body of Christ in accordance with one's own measure of faith."

PART II

Worship in Accord
with the Logos
(Romans 12:1)
Liturgy and Christology

ℰ℈

4

The Resurrection as the Foundation of Christian Liturgy: On the Meaning of Sunday for Christian Prayer and Christian Life

❧

We live under the observance of the Lord's Day,
the day on which our life has also risen"
—Ignatius of Antioch

WHAT IS THE ISSUE HERE?

It was the year 304, during the Diocletian persecution in North Africa, when Roman officials surprised a group of about fifty Christians who were attending the Sunday Eucharist to take them into custody. The transcript of the interrogations has been preserved. The proconsul said to the presbyter Saturninus: "By gathering all these together here you have acted against the orders of the emperors and the

73

caesars." The Christian redactor adds at this point that the presbyter's response was inspired by the Holy Spirit. He said: "Unconcerned about that (*securi*, 'completely secure'), we have been celebrating what is the Lord's." "What the Lord's is"—that is how I translate the Latin word *dominicus*. Its complex meaning can hardly be translated at all. First of all it denotes the Lord's Day, but at the same time it refers to the content of this day, to the sacrament of the Lord, to his resurrection and his presence in the eucharistic event. Let us return to the transcript: The proconsul insists on knowing why; the composed, superb response of the presbyter follows: "We have done this because that which is the Lord's cannot cease." Here the realization is unambiguously expressed that *the* Lord stands above *the* lords. Such knowledge lent the presbyter "security" (as he himself expressed it) precisely at the moment when it had become evident that the little Christian community was externally completely insecure and at the mercy of others.

Emeritus, the owner of the house where the Sunday celebration of the Eucharist had taken place, answered perhaps even more impressively. In response to the question of why he had permitted the forbidden gathering in his house he said first of all that those gathered were his brothers and he could not show them the door. Once again the proconsul was insistent. And there, in the second response, the real ground and motive come to light. "You had to forbid them entry," the proconsul had said. "I couldn't," answered Emeritus: "*Quoniam sine dominico non possumus*—for without the Day of the Lord, the mystery of the Lord, we cannot exist." The clear and decisive "we cannot" of the Christian conscience stands opposite the will of the caesars.[1] This phrase adopts the "we cannot be silent," the must of Christian preaching, used by Peter and John in response to the order of the Sanhedrin not to speak (Acts 4:20).

"Without the Day of the Lord we cannot exist." That is not arduous obedience toward a law of the Church felt to be external to oneself, but an expression of both interior necessity and desire. It points to that which has become the sustaining center of one's own existence, of one's entire being. It indicates something that has become so important that it must be done out of a feeling of great inner security and freedom, even at the risk of one's own life. For those speaking in this way it would obviously have appeared senseless to buy survival and outer peace by renouncing this foundation of life. They did not consider a casuistry that would have let worship appear to be dispensable as the lesser value when weighing the alternatives of Sunday obligation or a citizen's obligation, of Church law or the impending death sentence. For them it was not a case of choosing between *one* law and *another*, but of choosing between the meaning that sustains life and a meaningless life. At this point we can also understand the words of St. Ignatius of Antioch which appear as a motto at the beginning of this chapter. "We live according to the Lord's Day on which our life has also risen. How could we ever live without it?"[2]

Such a witness from the dawn of Church history could easily give rise to nostalgic reflections if one contrasts it with the lack of enthusiasm for Sunday service typical of the middle-European Christian. Granted, the Sunday crisis did not just start in our time. It already becomes apparent at the point when the *inner necessity* of Sunday is no longer felt: Instead of "without Sunday we cannot exist," Sunday obligation appears only as an imposed Church law, an *external necessity*. Then, like all duties coming from the outside, it is cropped more and more until only the requirement remains to have to attend a half-hour ritual that is becoming ever more remote. Asking when and why one can be excused from it ultimately becomes more important than asking why one should regularly celebrate it. Consequently, in the end it does not take much for one to stay away without any excuse at all.

Since the meaning of Sunday has so completely degenerated into a positivistic façade the question of whether the

Lord's Day is still really such an important topic in our age arises for us as well, the question of whether there are not really much more important themes for Christians, and especially for Christians in a world rent by the danger of war and social problems. In private we also sometimes ask ourselves if we are not simply pursuing the survival of our "club," the justification of our own profession by insisting on the Lord's Day.

The more profound question lying behind this is whether the Church is really only "our club" or God's original idea whose realization determines the fate of the world. On the other hand, with nostalgic comparisons between the past and today we would be doing justice neither to the witness of the martyrs nor to reality today. Even while being aware of all the necessary self-criticism we should not overlook the fact that there are still very many Christians today who would respond from a feeling of innermost security just like the early Christians. Without the Lord's Day we cannot exist; that which is the Lord's must not cease. On the other side of the issue we know that already during the New Testament period there was cause for complaining about poor church attendance (Heb. 10:25); this complaint appears again and again in the works of the Church Fathers. It seems to me that the real, albeit misunderstood and for the most part unrecognized, driving force behind the restlessness of today's leisure-time activities, behind the escape from everyday life and the pursuit of something completely different is the yearning for that which the martyrs called *dominicus*, that is, the longing for an encounter which makes life arise in us; it is the pursuit of what Christians received and are receiving on Sunday. Our question is: How can we show this to the people who seek it, and how can we find it again ourselves? Before we look for solutions and applications, which are without doubt also very necessary, I think that we ourselves must again arrive at an inner understanding of what the Lord's Day is.

THE THEOLOGY OF THE LORD'S DAY

Let us begin with the simplest matter. First, Sunday is a particular day of the week, the first day according to Jewish numbering, which was adopted by the Christians. Here we immediately run into something that seems to us to be positivistic and external, so we ask: Why should we not celebrate on Friday in Islamic countries, on Saturday where the majority are Jewish, and then on some other day somewhere else? Why should each person not be able to pick his or her day according to the rhythm of their work or way of life? What led to specifying this day anyhow? Is it just an agreement to make it possible for us at least to celebrate together? Or is there more to it than that?

To begin with, behind Sunday, the first day, there is another New Testament formula for the date which has also been adopted in the Credo of the Church: "He was raised on the third day in accordance with the scriptures" (1 Cor. 15:4). In the earliest scriptural tradition the *third* day was recorded and hence the memory of the discovery of the empty tomb and the first appearances of the Risen One preserved.[3] At the same time—and this is why "in accordance with the scriptures" is added—we are reminded that the third day was the day specified by the Scriptures, that is, by the Old Testament itself, for this fundamental event of world history—or, rather, not of world history but marking the escape from world history, the escape from the history of death and killing, the breakthrough and onset of a new life.

The concrete memory of the day is likewise interpreted by the designation "third day." In the Old Testament accounts describing the making of the covenant on Sinai, the third day is each time the day of theophany, that is, the day on which God reveals himself and speaks.[4] Accordingly, the time description "on the third day" marks Jesus' resurrection as the definitive event of the covenant, as the ultimate and real entry into history of God, who lets himself be touched in the middle of our world—a "God you can put your hands on," as we would say today. The resurrection means that God has retained power in history, that he has not relinquished it to the laws of nature. It means that he has not become powerless in the world of matter and matter-determined life. It means that the law of all laws, the universal law of death, is not the world's final power after all and that it does not have the last word. The last one is and remains he who is also the first one.

There is real theophany in the world. This is what the phrase "the third day" says. And it has occurred in such a way that God himself has restored the disturbed nature of justice and has established justice, justice not only for the living or for a still uncertain future generation, but justice extending beyond death, justice for *the* Dead One and for the dead, justice for all. Hence theophany has occurred in this event in which one has come back from death or, better put, gone beyond death. It has occurred through the reception of the body into eternity, proving that it, too, is capable of the eternal, capable of divinity. Jesus has not died and somehow or other gone to God, as people now and then say today, expressing indirectly their despair of God's actual power and of Jesus' actual resurrection in only a feigned demonstration of devotion. For behind this phrase is in truth their fear that they would be stepping on the toes of the natural sciences if they were to include the real body of Jesus in God's powerful actions and consider real time to be affected by God's might.

If this were the case, however, we would be denying that matter has the capacity to be saved. We would also be denying that humans have this capacity since they are, after all, a combination of matter and spirit. It seems to me that the theories which emphasize the wholeness of the human being in a seemingly superb way and thus speak of the whole death and the wholly new corporeal life are in fact barely disguised dualistic theories which invent unknown matter in order to remove reality itself from the sphere of theology, that is, from the sphere of God's speaking and acting. Resurrection means, however, that God says yes to *the whole* and that he *can* do this. In the resurrection God brings the approval of the seventh day of creation, his saying that all is good, to completion. The sin of humans has tried to make God into a liar. It has concluded that his creation is not good at all or that it is really only good for dying. Resurrection means that through the twisted paths of sin and more powerfully than sin God ultimately says: "It *is* good." God speaks his definitive "good" to creation by taking it up into himself and thus changing it into a permanence beyond all transcience.

At this point the connection between Sunday and the Eucharist becomes apparent. If the situation is as described, then the resurrection is not one event in a flood of others, an event that is followed by another and gradually slips back further and further into the past. Resurrection is the start of a present, a now that will never end. We often live at a great distance from this present. We separate ourselves all the more the more we stick to the merely transient, the more we turn our lives away from that which has proved itself on the cross and in the resurrection to be the real present in the midst of what passes by: the love that finds itself in losing itself. *It* remains present. The Eucharist is the present, the now of the Risen One who continually gives himself in the signs of the sacrifice and is our life in this way. For this reason the Eucharist is itself and as such the Day of the Lord: *dominicus*, as the martyrs of North Africa put it in one single word.

At the same time, the connection between Sunday and creational faith becomes evident here. The third day after Jesus' death is the first day of the week, the day of creation on which God said: "Let there be light!" Where belief in the resurrection keeps its New Testament wholeness and concreteness, Sunday and the meaning of Sunday can never be locked into mere history, into the history of the Christian community and its paschal celebration. Matter is involved here; creation is involved; the first day is involved, which Christians also call the eighth day: the restoration of all things. The Old and New Testaments cannot be separated, especially not in the interpretation of Sunday. Creation and faith cannot be detached from each other, least of all at the core of the Christian profession.[5]

For a variety of reasons theologians often have a kind of phobia about treating the topic of creation. This, however, leads to the degeneration of faith into a kind of parochial ideology, to the worldlessness of faith and the godlessness of the world, which is life-threatening for both. Where creation shrinks to the world around us, human beings and the world are out of kilter. But there is a complaint resounding ever more audibly out of this creation which has degenerated into mere environment, and precisely this complaint should tell us once more that the creature is in fact reaching out for the appearance of the children of God.

SABBATH AND SUNDAY

The Problem

At this point the question about the relationship between the Sabbath and Sunday appears. It is a disputed question for which there is no uniform answer in the New Testament. Only in the course of the fourth century and at the beginning of the fifth did a solution gradually begin to take shape which was then generally accepted, but which is once more being vehemently challenged today. According to the unanimous witness of the Synoptic tradition, Jesus himself repeatedly came into conflict with the Jewish Sabbath observance of his time. He opposed it vigorously as a misunderstanding of God's law. Paul took up this line of argument; his battle for freedom from the law was also a battle against the constraints of the Jewish calendar of feasts, including the Sabbath obligations. We encounter an echo of this confrontation in the text of St. Ignatius of Antioch, which is guiding us: "Whoever has gone from life under the old rules to the new, to hope, is no longer a follower of the Sabbath, but lives according to the Day of the Lord." The rhythm of the Sabbath and this "living-by-the-Day-of-the-Lord" confront each other as two fundamentally different life-styles, the former as a state of being lodged in particular sets of ordinances and the latter as life from what is to come, from hope.

But how did the transition from the observance of the Sabbath to the celebration of Sunday actually take place? We may accept as certain that already in the apostolic age the day of the resurrection had established itself entirely on its own merit as the day of Christian gathering. This was the "Lord's Day" (Rev. 1:10), on which he appeared among his followers and they went to meet him. To assemble around the Risen One meant that he was once again breaking bread for his followers (Luke 24:30, 35). It was an encounter with Christ here and now, a moving toward his Second Coming, and simultaneously the presence of the cross as his true exaltation, as the occasion on which his love spreads. The New Testament as well as the earliest manuscripts from the second century confirm this beyond all doubt: Sunday is the day of worship for Christians.[6] It has assimilated the ritualistic meaning of the Sabbath and at the same time represents the transformation of the old cult into the new, which is precisely what has occurred through the cross and the resurrection. But also the connection with the theme of creation, which is fundamental for the Sabbath, was explicit in a changed form through the designation of the first day of the week, that is, the day creation began. The resurrection connects the beginning and the end, creation and restoration. In the magnificent hymn to Christ in Colossians, Christ is presented as the firstborn of all creation (1:15) as well as the firstborn from the dead (1:18), through whom God wanted to reconcile all things to himself. It is precisely here that we find the synthesis which lay hidden in the designation of the first day and which should shape the theology of Sunday in the future. In this respect it was possible for the whole theological content of the Sabbath to pass into the Sunday celebration of Christians in a renewed way; indeed, the passage from the Sabbath to Sunday reflects precisely the continuity and innovation of what is Christian.

Admittedly, the most important practical characteristic of the Sabbath could not at first be transferred to Sunday—its social function as a day of rest and freedom from servile work. Since Christianity was classified by state law in the first three centuries as an unauthorized religion, open celebration of Sunday was not possible. In the Jewish-Christian milieu this role of the Sabbath remained, and it certainly continued to be kept there in this sense. We do not know in detail what the situation in the pagan world was in this regard. It is notable that after the conversion of Constantine, that is, in the fourth century, we do encounter the celebration of both days (Sunday and Sabbath) in various sources. As examples I would like to quote two texts from the so-called *Apostolic Constitutions*. One text states: "Spend the Sabbath and the Lord's Day in festive joy since the one is the commemoration of creation, the other the commemoration of the resurrection!"[7] Somewhat later it says: "I Paul and I Peter order: Slaves should work five days, but on the Sabbath and the Lord's Day they should have time for instruction in the faith of the Church. For the Sabbath has its foundation in creation, the Lord's Day in the resurrection."[8] Perhaps the same author who speaks here under the pseudonym "I Paul and I Peter" also put himself in the shoes of St. Ignatius of Antioch and created a longer version of the *Letter to the Magnesians*, from which we have taken our motto. In this longer version he is concerned with toning down the fierce attack against the "followers of the Sabbath." So he writes under the name of the renowned bishop of Antioch as follows:

> Let us therefore not observe the Sabbath in the Jewish manner any more, deriving pleasure from idleness, then "whoever does not work should not eat" (2 Thess. 3:10). . . . Rather, each of you should observe the Sabbath in a spiritual way. You should

derive pleasure from studying the law and not from resting the body. You should marvel at God's creation and not eat stale food, drink tepid liquids, walk a marked path and delight in dancing and senseless racket![9]

The extent to which such texts are representative of the situation of Christianity at large is an open question. In any case, after the early clashes about differentiating the specifically Christian and about its uniqueness and importance, there emerge an effort to emphasize what is special about both days—the Sabbath and Sunday—and also an effort to show the compatibility of both traditions and make room for both of them in the life of a Christian. We find the same basic orientation in Gregory of Nyssa when he says that the two days "have become siblings."[10] Granted, he draws different conclusions from the related meaning of the two days than the *Apostolic Constitutions:* there is no longer a compelling reason for dividing the spiritual content shared by the siblings between two days. It can be put into one single day, but the day of Jesus Christ must then necessarily take precedence. This day is simultaneously the third, the first, and the eighth day, the expression of Christian uniqueness and the expression of the Christian synthesis of all realities.[11]

Also crucial for working out this synthesis had been the fact that the Sabbath is part of the decalogue. In Paul, even with all the polemic against the law, it had always remained clear that the decalogue stays in full force as the form of the double commandment to love and that through it Christians retain the Law and the Prophets in their entirety, in their true depth.[12] On the other hand, it was also clear that the decalogue had to be read in a new way, from Christ's perspective, and that it had to be understood in the Holy Spirit. This made it possible to give Christians the freedom of dropping the Sabbath as a specific day and including it in the Day of the Lord. This also had to give them the freedom to understand the meaning and the form of the Sabbath in a deeper way than the casuistry fought by Jesus and Paul had done. But it also had to entail the imperative to grasp and to fulfill the true meaning of the Sabbath.

The Theology of the Sabbath

The question therefore also arises for us with a certain degree of urgency: What is this real and valid content of the Sabbath? To answer this question in a suitable way we would have to interpret the fundamental texts on the Sabbath in the Old Testament with care, that is, not only the creation account (Gen. 2:1ff.) but also the legal texts from Exodus (e.g., 20:8–11; 31:12–17) and Deuteronomy (e.g., 5:15; 12:9) as well as the texts of the prophetic tradition (e.g., Ezek. 20:12). To do all this cannot be my aim here; instead I would like to try to focus briefly on three main points.

1. To start with, it is fundamental that the Sabbath is part of the story of creation. One could actually say that the metaphor of the seven-day week was selected for the creation account because of the Sabbath. By culminating in the sign of the covenant, the Sabbath, the creation account clearly shows that creation and covenant belong together from the start, that the Creator and the Redeemer can only be one and the same God. It shows that the world is not a neutral receptacle where human beings then accidentally became involved, but that right from the start creation came to be so that there would be a place for the covenant. But it also shows that the covenant can exist only if it conforms to the yardstick of creation. From this starting point a merely historical religion or simple salvation history without metaphysics is just as unthinkable as a worldless piety that contents itself with private happiness, the private salvation of one's soul or the escape into an amiably active parish community.

Thus, the Sabbath calls first of all for deep respect and gratitude toward the Creator and his creation. If the creation story somehow describes the establishment of a cult as well, then this means in any case that the cult in both its form and matter is necessarily connected to creation. It means that the things of creation are at God's disposal and that we can and must ask him for them. On the other hand, it means that we must not forget God's right of ownership when we use the things of the world. It means that these things were not handed over to us for arbitrary domination, but were given to us from the measure of the true ruler and owner for a dominion of service. Wherever the Sabbath or Sunday is cherished, creation is cherished as well.

2. A second aspect is connected to this. The Sabbath is the day of God's freedom and the day of human participation in God's freedom. Reflecting on Israel's liberation from slavery is central to the Sabbath theme, which is, however, much more than commemoration. The Sabbath is not simply remembrance of what has passed but an active exercise of freedom. This fundamental content is the reason why the Sabbath should be a day of rest to an equal degree for humans and animals, for masters and servants. The legislation for the Jubilee Year shows that we are concerned with more than just a regulation of free time. In the Jubilee Year all the proprietary relationships return to their origin and all the forms of subjugation that had been built up through time come to an end.[13]

The great Sabbath of the festival year thus reveals what the objective of every Sabbath is: anticipation of the society free of domination, a foretaste of the city to come. On the Sabbath there are no masters and no servants; there is only the freedom of all the children of God and creation's release from anxiety. What the social theorist regards as the utopia of a world that can never be formed is a concrete demand on the Sabbath: the reciprocal freedom and equality of all creatures. For this reason the Sabbath is the heart of social legislation. If all social subordinations are suspended on the first or the seventh day, and if all social arrangements are revised in the rhythm of seven times seven years, then they will always be relative to the mutual freedom and common ownership of all. The book of Chronicles even teaches us that Israel's exile occurred because she ignored the regulations of the Jubilee Year, the great Sabbath, and hence disregarded the basic law of creation and of the Creator. Looking back, all other sins seem secondary in the face of this fundamental unfaithfulness, in the face of this locking oneself into the self-made world of work which negates God's sovereignty.[14]

3. The third element of the theology of the Sabbath is revealed here, its eschatological dimension. The Sabbath is the anticipation of the messianic hour, not only in thoughts and desires but in concrete action. Only by living according to the form of the messianic age do we open up the doors of the world for the time of the Messiah. We also become practiced in the way of life of the world to come. Irenaeus would say: We are getting used to God's way of life just as he got used to us during his life as a human.

Thus, cultic, social, and eschatological dimensions permeate one another. The cult rooted in biblical faith is not an imitation of the course of the world in miniature—as is the case for the basic form of all cults of nature. It is an imitation of God himself and therefore a preliminary exercise in the world to come. Only in this way does one correctly understand the singularity of the biblical creation account. The pagan creation accounts on which the biblical story is in part based end without exception in the establishment of a cult, but the cult in this case is situated in the cycle of *do ut des*. The gods create humans in order to be fed by them; the humans need the gods to keep the course of the world in order. As I have already said, the biblical creation account, too, must definitely be seen, at least in a certain sense, as the establishment of a cult. But here cult means the liberation of humans through their participation in the freedom of God and thus the liberation of creation itself, its release into the freedom of the children of God.

The Christian Synthesis

If you read the dispute Jesus had concerning the Sabbath or St. Paul's polemic on the same subject in the light of this knowledge, then it becomes perfectly clear that in both cases the real significance of the Sabbath is not at issue. The point is instead to defend the essential meaning of the Sabbath as a feast of freedom over against a practice that has turned it into a day of nonfreedom. If Jesus, however, wanted not to abolish the real substance of the Sabbath but to save it, then a Christian theology that would like to remove it from Sunday is not on the right path. In his foundational investigations on the Sabbath and Sunday, W. Rordorf supports the view that combining the Sabbath and Sunday was a work of the period following Constantine's conversion; by saying this he has already passed judgment on this synthesis. He thinks that, apart from a few exceptions, the Christian churches have hitherto been stuck in the spell of this post-Constantinian synthesis and adds: "Since they must, for better or for worse, break with the old traditions of the Constantinian age, they will now be faced with the question of whether they can summon up the courage to rid themselves of the yoke of the Sabbath/ Sunday synthesis."[15] More recent Catholic statements sound even more radical. L. Brandolini, for example, maintains that the emergence of Sunday came about in strict opposition to the Jewish Sabbath, but that in the fourth century a countermovement arose that gradually resulted in making a Sabbath out of Sunday and thus led to a naturalistic, legalistic, and individualistic concept of cult.[16] As a result, reform is difficult today, especially since the Church is stuck in the Middle Ages and hardly seems capable of change in spite of Vatican II's efforts at renewal.[17]

Such reflections are correct insofar as the Christian Sunday is not tied to the state's exempting this day from work. Under no circumstances does Sunday correspond to a sociopolitical phenomenon that is attainable only under very special social conditions. In this respect the struggle to understand the deeper meaning of Sunday is justified since it exists independently of the fluctuations in external situations. But whoever deduces from this fact that the spiritual meaning of the Sabbath is completely opposed to that of Sunday has radically misunderstood both the Old Testament *and* the New Testament. The spiritualization of the Old Testament, which is part of the essence of the New, is at the same time an incarnation that is always new. It is not a retreat from society and not a retreat from creation, but a new and more profound way of penetrating them. As with all the major themes of theology, the issue of correctly determining the relationship between the Old and the New Testament proves to be fundamental here.

Today's theology often fluctuates between a Marcionism that would like to rid itself completely of the burden of the Old Testament and withdraw into the particularity of what is only inner-Christian and a return to a merely political and social interpretation of the biblical tradition lying behind the transition to the New Testament.[18] The synthesis of the Testaments worked out in the early Church corresponds solely to the fundamental intention of the New Testament message, and it alone can give Christianity its own historical force. If one rejects the aspect of creation and the social components along with the Old Testament—that is, in this case along with the Sabbath—then Christianity becomes a clublike pastime and liturgy turns into entertainment that still appears old-fashioned even when it is presented with all sorts of progressive decorations. By eliminating the world in such a way one loses the starting point for the Christian doctrine of freedom and consequently falsifies the Christian notion of worship, whose essential and basic pattern is seen in the creation account's structure of the week, a pattern that admittedly has received its dramatic content through the Pascha of Christ. This Passover of Christ, however, does not do away with the vision of the creation account but lends it its entire concreteness. Christian worship is the anticipation of communal freedom in which the human being imitates God, becomes the "image of God." It is possible to anticipate such freedom only because creation has been fashioned for its sake right from the beginning.

APPLICATIONS

At the close the practical questions are once more asking for a hearing with great urgency. At the same time, however, we should never lose sight of the fact that reflecting on theological truth is itself something quite practical. In his recently published autobiographical sketches, Romano Guardini movingly described how making the truth present seemed to him to be the most concrete and therefore the most pressing task of his age.[19] Because of this attitude he came into conflict with important figures who shared his moment during those years in Berlin, with Dr. Münch, at that time the chair of the Association of Academics, and with Dr. Sonnenschein, the distinguished Berlin university chaplain. Looking back, we have to say that each of these men attended to a necessary task and thus represented a necessary aspect of pastoral work. But if from the distance of half a century we could now reconcile what at that time clashed, we still have to recognize without excluding anyone that Guardini's passionate and unpremeditated effort simply to let the truth speak in the midst of the reign of lies had the most far-reaching effect and rapidly proved itself to be completely practical right up to the decisions of the Second Vatican Council. In the long run we will be able to have the greatest effect if we at first rely not on our own deeds but on the inner strength of truth, which we must learn to see and then let speak.

In conclusion I would like to tackle two of the most pressing practical issues from the perspective of the theological insights that have just been developed.

Priestless Sunday Services

As a consequence of these considerations, our actions in practice have to be guided by two principles.

1. The sacrament must take precedence over psychology. The Church must take precedence over the group.

2. Operating under the proviso of this hierarchy, the local churches must seek the right answer for each situation respectively, knowing that the salvation of all humans (the *salus animarum*) is their real mission. In this orientation of all their work both their obligation and their freedom are to be found.

Let us look at the two principles a little more closely. In mission countries, in the diaspora and in situations of persecution, it is not new that people cannot get to the celebration of the Eucharist on Sunday and that they must then try to take part in the Sunday of the Church to the degree that this is possible. In our part of the world, the decline of priestly vocations has noticeably given rise to such situations, to which we were largely unaccustomed until now. Unfortunately people have often covered up the search for the right answer with ideological theories on communality that stand in the way of the real concern rather than being of service to it. For example, it has been said: Every church that once had a pastor or at least regular Sunday worship should continue to be the place of assembly for the parish of that locality. Only in this way would the church remain the focal point of the village; only in this way would the parish stay alive as a parish. For this reason it is more important for the parish community to gather here and hear and celebrate the Word of God than to take advantage of the actually given possibility of participating in the eucharistic celebration in a church close by.

There is much here that is plausible and undoubtedly also well meant. But the fundamental evaluations of faith have been forgotten. In this way of looking at things the experience of togetherness and the fostering of the village community rank higher than the gift of the sacrament. The experience of community is, without doubt, more immediately accessible and more easily explained than the sacrament. So it seems reasonable to switch from the objectivity of the Eucharist to the subjectivity of experience, from the theological to the sociological and the psychological. But the results of placing the experience of community above sacramental reality in such a way are momentous. The congregation is now celebrating itself; the Church becomes a vehicle for social purposes; and at the same time she is promoting a romanticism that is somewhat anachronistic in our mobile society. To be sure, at the outset people are elated because they feel confirmed by the fact that they themselves are celebrating in their church, that they can "do it alone." But soon they notice that there is *only* the entity of their own making—that they no longer receive but merely present themselves. Then, however, the whole thing becomes superfluous because the Sunday service basically goes no further than what they normally and always do anyhow. It no longer touches any other order; it, too, is just their own thing. For this reason, that unconditional "must" which the Church had always spoken about cannot be inherent to this service. But then, according to an inner logic, this evaluation expands to include the real celebration of the Eucharist as well. For if the Church herself seems to be saying that assembly is more important than Eucharist, then the Eucharist is also just "assembly"—otherwise it would not be possible to treat them as equivalents. The whole Church then sinks into what is self-made and Durkheim's sad vision is proven right, namely, that religion and cult in general are only forms of social stabilization through the self-portrayal of a society. But once you know this, this stabilization no longer functions since it only works when you think there is more at stake. Whoever elevates the community to the level of an end in itself is precisely the one who dissolves its foundations. What seems to be so pious and reasonable at the beginning is actually a radical inversion of the important concerns and categories in which we eventually achieve the opposite of what was intended. Only when the sacrament retains its unconditional character and its absolute priority over all communal purposes and all spiritually edifying intentions does it build community and "edify" humans. Even if a sacramental liturgy had fewer psychological trappings and were subjectively more lackluster and duller (if one may speak in such a purpose-oriented way) it is still "socially" more effective in the long run than the self-edification of a parish community performed with psychological and sociological expertise. We are concerned, namely, with the fundamental question of whether something happens here that does not come from us or whether we alone plan and shape the community ourselves. If there is not the higher "must" of the sacrament, the freedom that we claim for ourselves becomes empty since it has been robbed of its content.

Things are completely different when there is a real emergency. If we have a priestless Sunday service in this situation, we are no longer turning to something that is simply of our own making; this service is rather the collective gesture with which we reach out for *dominicus*, the Sunday of the Church. With this action we are holding on to the shared "must" and "want to" of the Church and thus holding on to the Lord himself. The crucial question is: Where is the boundary between what we merely want and what is real necessity? Certainly this boundary cannot be clearly drawn in the abstract, and even in each case it will be fluid again and again. In separate situations it must be set in agreement with the bishop on the basis of the pastoral sensitivity of those affected. There are rules that can help. It is not an explicit precept of canon law that a priest may not celebrate Mass more than three times on Sunday, but it does correspond to the limits of what he can possibly do.

This arrangement has to do with the celebrant; on behalf of the faithful the questions to ask are whether the distance to travel is reasonable and whether the services are available at suitable times. We should not create too much prefabricated casuistry out of this, but leave room for conscientious decision making in view of what each situation requires. It is important that the weights remain correctly distributed and that the Church is not celebrating herself but the Lord whom she receives in the Eucharist and toward whom she moves in those situations in which the priestless parish reaches out for his gift.

Weekend Culture and the Christian Sunday

In my opinion it is far more realistic in our part of the world to turn the question around: What do we do when our parish communities leave their places of residence on Friday evening or Saturday in great haste only to show up again after the last Sunday service is long since over? How can we reconcile weekend culture and Sunday with each other? How can we again relate leisure time to the greater freedom we should be practicing on the Day of the Lord? I think we will have to have more ideas on this subject than we have had up till now—on the one hand concerning the mobility of pastoral work and the mutual openness of the parishes to one another; on the other hand concerning ways to make the parish community an inner home prior to what goes on in worship, a home that absorbs industrial society's compulsion to get away and gives it another goal. I am of the opinion that all the getaways we witness may be directed at diversion, relaxation, encounter, and liberation from the toils of everyday life, but that behind these totally legitimate desires there is still a deeper yearning: the longing to find a real home in brotherly communion and to experience a real contrast, that is, the longing for something "totally other" in the face of the glut caused by the immense scale of all we have made.

The Sunday liturgy should be responding to this. It will

come off badly if it wants to enter the competition of show business. A pastor is not an emcee, and the liturgy is not a variety show. It will also come off badly if it wants to be a sort of engaging circle of friends. That can perhaps develop subsequent to the liturgy and out of encounters that have evolved there. But the liturgy itself must be more. It must become clear that a dimension of existence opens up here that we are all secretly seeking: the presence of that which cannot be made—theophany, mystery, and in it God saying that all is good, his approval, which reigns over being and is alone capable of making it good so that it can be accepted by us in the midst of all the tensions and suffering.[20]

We have to find the happy medium between a ritualism in which the liturgical action is performed in an unintelligible and nonrelational manner by the priest and a craze for understandability which in the end dissolves the whole into the work of human beings and robs it of its Catholic dimension and of the objectivity of mystery. Through the community that believes and believingly understands, the liturgy must have its own luminosity which then becomes a call and hope for those who do not believe and therefore do not understand. As *opus dei* it must be the place where all *opera hominum* come to an end and are transcended and thus the place where a new freedom dawns, which we seek in vain in the liberties of the entertainment industry.

In such a way the liturgy, in accordance with the essential meaning of Sunday, could again become a place of freedom that is more than free time and permissiveness. This true freedom, however, is the one we are all on the lookout for.

NOTES

1. The patristic texts on the subject of the Sabbath and Sunday have been collected by W. Rordorf, *Sabbat und Sonntag in der Alten Kirche*, Traditio christiana 2 (Zurich, 1972). The text quoted here is from the "Acta ss Saturnini et aliorum . . . ," no. 109, p. 176.

2. *Magnesians* 9:1,2, in Rordorf, *Sabbath,* no. 78, p. 134 [translated into English from the German].

3. See J. Blank, *Paulus und Jesus* (Munich, 1968), pp. 154ff. Blank summarizes the result of his very careful analysis on p. 156 as follows: "'On the third day' is the specification of a day in agreement with the earliest Christian tradition in the Gospels and refers to the discovery of the empty tomb; as with the statement about his death, the 'in accordance with the scriptures' refers to Isa 53:10f." For this reason it is exegetically and theologically completely groundless when R. Heinzmann accuses the *Catechism* of a "naïve scriptural fundamentalism" because it also considers the third day to be—first and foremost—a historical measure of time from the burial of Jesus to the discovery of the empty tomb; see "Was ist der Mensch? Anfragen an das Menschenbild des *Katechismus der katholischen Kirche*," in *Ein Katechismus für die Welt*, ed. E. Schulz (Düsseldorf, 1994), pp. 97–98. In his polemic against the *Catechism* Heinzmann wrongly refers to K. Lehmann, *Auferweckt am dritten Tag nach der Schrift*, 2nd ed. (Freiburg, 1969). Lehmann tried to clarify the theological significance of the third day from the sources, which is what Paul is asking for when he says that the third day was the time of the resurrection "in accordance with the scriptures"; with that he is expressly making two claims: this is a real day and this day has theological significance. Such a concurrence between factuality and meaning is contradictory only for a person who can see no meaning in the fact and nothing actually realized in the meaning, that is, who sees history as simple, empirical fact deprived of God's direction. Furthermore, although written in completely different linguistic styles and from a different starting point, the resurrection accounts in all four Gospels uniformly give the third day as the point in time for the discovery of the empty tomb and the first appearances of the Risen One—in spite of all their other differences. They all say that Friday, the eve of the great Sabbath, is the day of Jesus' death; they all mention the rest period of the Sabbath (taken for granted in Jewish areas); and they all say that on the first day of the week the walk to the grave took place and the discovery of the empty tomb and the first encounters with Christ, the Risen One, occurred. Whereas Jesus' prophecies of his passion (cf. Mark 8:31; 9:31; 10:34; Luke 9:22; 24:7) and 1 Cor. 15:4 use the formula of the third day, these accounts of the resurrection mention the first day of the week. From this specification of the day, the Sunday gathering for the Lord's Supper developed in apostolic times. Whoever blocks out the facts here and withdraws into the mere "theological" not only undermines Sunday for Christians, but also takes the body from

the resurrection and thus destroys the foundation of Christian faith as a whole.

4. Cf. especially Exod. 19:11,16. I have tried to describe the contexts in more detail in my little book *Der Gott Jesu Christi* (Munich, 1976), pp. 76–84 [Eng.: *The God of Jesus Christ* (Franciscan Press, 1978)]; cf. also J. Ratzinger, *Suchen, was droben ist* (Freiburg, 1985), pp. 40ff. [Eng.: *Seek That Which Is Above* (San Francisco: Ignatius Press, 1986)].

5. Concerning the patristic symbolism of the first, third, seventh, and eighth days, see J. Daniélou, *Liturgie und Bibel* (Munich, 1963), pp. 225–305 [Eng.: *The Bible and the Liturgy* (London, 1956)]; K. H. Schwarte, *Die Vorgeschichte der augustinischen Weltalterlehre* (Bonn, 1966; very instructive on the patristic view of the connection between creation and salvation history); brief information can also be found in H. Auf der Maur, *Feiern im Rhythmus der Zeit*, Gottesdienst der Kirche: Handbuch der Liturgiewissenschaft, 5, 1 (Regensburg, 1983), pp. 26-49; interesting comments can also be found in W. Rordorf, "Le dimanche—source et plénitude du temps liturgique chrétien," *Cristianesimo nella storia* 5 (1984): 1–9.

6. For the documentary evidence, see W. Rordorf, *Sabbat und Sonntag* (see n. 1), pp. 27–87.

7. *Apostolic Constitutions* 7.23.3, in Rordorf, *Sabbath und Sonntag*, no. 58, p. 100. [This and all the following quotations from Rordorf have been translated into English from the German.] The *Apostolic Constitutions* are a collection of Church legislation dating from the fourth century; see H. Rahner, "Apostolische Konstitutionen," *Lexikon für Theologie und Kirche*, 2nd ed. (1957), 1:759.

8. *Apostolic Constitutions* 8.33.; in Rordorf, *Sabbat und Sonntag*.

9. Pseudo-Ignatius, *Ad Magn.* 9, in Rordorf, *Sabbat und Sonntag*, no. 59, p. 102.

10. Gregory of Nyssa, "Adv. eos qui castigationes aegre ferunt" (*PG* 46:309 B–C, in Rordorf, *Sabbat und Sonntag*, no. 52, pp. 92-93): "You who did not cherish the Sabbath, with what kind of eyes do you regard the Lord's Day? Or do you not know that these days are siblings (*adelphai*)?"

11. On this point, see the superb turn of phrase with which an anonymous homily (ascribed to Athanasius) probably from the close of the fourth century summarizes and definitively expresses in a more precise way the outcome of the struggle of the patristic period to state the relationship between the Sabbath and Sunday: *metethēke de ho kyrios tēn tou sabbatou hēmeran eis kyriakēn* ("the Lord has transferred the Sabbath to his day"), in Rordorf, *Sabbat und Sonntag*, no. 64, pp. 110–11.

12. See H. Gese, *Zur biblischen Theologie* (Munich, 1977), pp. 54–84; here one finds important information concerning the genuine meaning of the Sabbath in the Old Testament and its adoption by Jesus. Cf. also Rordorf, *Sabbat und Sonntag*, pp. xiif.

13. See Th. Maertens, *Heidnisch-jüdische Wurzeln christlicher Feste* (Mainz, 1965), pp. 114–47, 150–59. Maertens, however, does give one-sided prominence to the aspect of "spiritualization" in the transition from the Old Testament to the New Testament and overlooks the fact that Christian "spiritualization" is incarnation and christological concentration.

14. 2 Chron. 36:21.

15. W. Rordorf, *Sabbat und Sonntag* (see n. 1), p. xx.

16. L. Brandolini, "Domenica," in *Nuovo dizionario di liturgia*, ed. D. Sartore and M. Triacca (Rome, 1984), pp. 377–95 (quotation from p. 385f.).

17. Ibid., p. 379; cf. p. 386.

18. On this point, see what is said about the inversion of symbols in the Instruction of the Congregation of Faith *de quibusdam rationibus "Theologiae Liberationis"* from August 6, 1984, X:14–16, in *Congregatio pro Doctrina Fidei, Documenta inde a Concilio Vaticano secundo expleto edita (1966–1985)* (Libr. Ed. Vaticana, 1985), p. 279.

19. R. Guardini, *Berichte über mein Leben: Autobiographische Aufzeichnungen* (Düsseldorf, 1984), pp. 109–13. See especially p. 109: "At the same time, the longer I worked, the less I was concerned about the immediate effect. Right from the start, at first instinctively, but then more and more consciously, I wanted to make the truth shine. Truth is a power; but only if you do not demand an immediate effect from it." Also moving is the statement on pp. 114ff.: "Here [at the talks in St. Canisius Church in Charlottenburg] I experienced perhaps most intensely what I said above about the power of truth. I have rarely been so conscious of how great and how fundamentally true and in control of life the message of Catholic Christianity is as on those evenings. At times it was as if the truth were standing in the room like a living being." Similarly expressed on p. 110.

20. For this reason the theory propagated on several occasions that the liturgy can only be celebrated with a priest one knows and in a parish where the parishioners know one another is wrong. Here the liturgy quite clearly sinks to the level of a social ritual. The wonderful thing about Catholicism, after all, is that believers are not strangers to one another and that wherever faith is present each one of the faithful is at home.

"Built from Living Stones": The House of God and the Christian Way of Worshiping God

෴

THE BIBLICAL MESSAGE ABOUT THE TEMPLE MADE FROM LIVING STONES

The phrase "living stones" is taken from the First Letter of Peter; its meaning, however, pervades the entire New Testament—it is characteristic of the way the hope of the Old Covenant is transformed and intensified in the face of the crucified and risen Jesus Christ. The verses in the Letter of Peter referring to the spiritual house built from living stones belong to a textual unit that may be regarded as an early baptismal catechesis, as an introduction to the Christian faith in which the inner claim of the process experienced by a person in baptism is interpreted.[1] According to these verses, it belongs to the fundamental content of this process that baptized Christians are fitted into a growing edifice that has Christ as its foundational stone. Various motifs run together here. The words from the Psalter about the stone that was rejected by the builders (Ps. 118:22) are incorporated. In the prayer of Israel this was a message of comfort and hope during the trying experiences of her history. The rejected stone that became the cornerstone was Israel herself—the people who counted for nothing in the game of the powers who created history, the people who were thoughtlessly cast aside and did not seem to belong anywhere except to the building rubble of world history. Standing before their God they knew that the mystery of election reigned over them and that they were in reality the cornerstone. But in the fate of Jesus Christ, these words were then fulfilled in a completely unexpected way. Oddly enough, the psalm from which they are taken, Psalm 118, had also been messianically interpreted in early Judaism, but it had not occurred to anyone to deduce from this that the Messiah would suffer. On the contrary, according to this exegesis the coming of the Messiah spelled the realization of the triumphant message found in these verses: through him Israel would finally arise from the rubble and become the cornerstone. But when the Bible is read anew in a dialogue with the risen Christ, the phrase about the rejected stone appears as a prophecy of suffering, a prediction of the crucified Christ who became the cornerstone from the cross and *in this way* made Israel the cornerstone. Two phrases from Isaiah (28:16 and 8:14) that were also integrated into the early Christian catechesis reinforce this view. All these texts, however, ultimately say the same thing: becoming a Christian means becoming part of the building erected on the rejected stone. They speak of the passion and the glory of the Church, which is always subject to the law of the castaway stone. Precisely in this way the Church fulfills the dream of hope, which ultimately supports all human construction. The building done by humans aims at the construction of a place to stay; it seeks security, a home, freedom. It is a declaration of war against death, against insecurity, against fear, against loneliness. For this reason the desire of humans to build is fulfilled in the temple, in that building into which they invite God. The temple is the expression of the human longing to have God as a fellow occupant, the longing to be able to reside with God and thus to experience the perfect way of living, the consummate community, which banishes loneliness and fear once and for all. The idea of the temple is really the cohesive motif in the various verses about the stone that are found in the First Letter of Peter and in related New Testament texts. After the horrible catastrophe of Jerusalem in which the people, in a terrible misunderstanding of the Promise and under the impression that God would ultimately defend his residence, had turned the temple into the site of a vicious battle right up into the Holy of Holies—after this catastrophe Christianity really knew what it had actually known since the cross and resurrection anyway: that the true temple of God is built from living stones. It knows that the true temple of God has not been destroyed and that it is in fact indestructible. It knows that God himself erects this temple and that the primordial dream of God dwelling among his people is fulfilled in those who trust in the rejected stone—they themselves are the temple.

Old Testament Roots

The few sentences that mention the living stones in 1 Peter therefore include an account that has come a long way, and they show the new slant Christian faith has given this account. In order to clarify what is audible here—the understanding of God's presence in the world, of his dwelling among humans, and the understanding of Church and Christian existence that this entails, I would like to examine to some extent at least two stages of the path taken for granted in this text. First of all we must look back at the beginning of the temple in Israel. After fighting many battles, David has finally been able to secure the realm. His monarchy is unchallenged; he lives in a palace built of cedar. Israel has overcome the period of her unsettledness, her wandering, and her homelessness and is now permanently housed in the promised land. Her God, however, continues to dwell in the tabernacle, as he did during the time Israel wandered in the desert—he has remained a homeless, a wandering God, so to speak. David senses the contradiction here, the anachronistic nature of this state of affairs in which two stages of civilization exist side by side—in which God has been left behind in the nomadic phase and should now be brought into that which has been newly attained. He wants to build God an appropriate house, and at first he finds himself encouraged by the prophet Nathan. But then, before long, the word of God comes to Nathan with a new directive, which states: "Are you the one to build me a house to live in? . . . The Lord declares to you that the Lord will make *you* a house." (2 Sam. 7:5, 11). In these verses a breakthrough and radical change in the religious history of humanity appear on the scene, whose dimensions would become clear only centuries later. In principle the change has already occurred here but admittedly still required the passion of Jesus the Son.

Humans do not build a house for God; God builds a house for humans. God himself executes God's building. What the house built by God consists of becomes clear in the subsequent verses of Nathan's prophecy: it consists of people. It consists in the kingdom remaining in the house of David forever. It consists in God's grace being more powerful than all the sins of this house. The house of David will be punished for its sins, but it will not be destroyed. Through all the decline and decay it stands; God builds it up. Here it is predicted that David's kingdom and his house, which will become God's own building, will last forever. For the first time the features emerge of that son of David who endures all the sin of the world and in whom the greater power of grace is living presence. David does not build; God builds. Through all the destruction of sin and guilt, God, in indestructible graciousness, builds a kingdom by means of which he himself

reigns and dwells among his people. God remains the homeless one for whom every building of stone is too small and
who in spite of this finds room in humans, especially in
humans. His indwelling transpires in grace which builds. It is
perhaps seldom that one can grasp the inner unity of the Testaments as palpably as in this bold scene of the prophecy of
Nathan. Compared with this central point of view, the temple of Solomon along with its successors has only "come in
in-between," to adopt a phrase of St. Paul. A verse in the
Nathan prophecy definitely refers to it as well; here we can
leave the question aside whether this verse has come from a
later theological redaction, as prominent Old Testament
exegetes assume, or whether it is original.[2] With regard to the
real issue, it is in any case peripheral to the main drift of the
prophecy, referring to an intermediate solution that was
unavoidable, but which must remain an intermediate solution
and not become the goal of the Promise. God cannot simply
be housed like a human on a new cultural level as if he also
had to go through the stages of human development. The
homelessness of the nomadic years has made him known
more accurately than the housing of the advanced civilization
that wanted to hold him captive in the human dimensions.

New Testament Fulfillment

Only against this background can the New Testament scene
of the cleansing of the temple be understood correctly, which,
according to what the evangelists imply, became the definitive
starting point of Jesus' passion but which at the same time
also decisively helped to bring to light the true depth of his
mission. Without this incident, the different sayings about the
building and the living stones would not have arisen.[3] In general the account of the expulsion of the money changers and
sheep and cattle dealers from the holy precinct is understood
much too innocuously. We have the impression that Jesus
acted in holy anger much like someone who would pounce on

the sellers of devotional objects and denounce their improper linking of faith and business. But it is not quite that simple. In the temple district the Roman currency with its images of pagan gods or deified emperors could not be used; exchange bureaus were therefore needed to convert the secular currency into the currency of the temple. This was a completely legitimate practice just like the one of providing animals that were needed for worship in the temple and were sacrificed there. What Jesus does is of a very fundamental nature. It follows along the lines of the momentous words to the Samaritan woman: the true worshipers will worship in spirit and truth (John 4:23)—not on Mount Gerizim, nor on Mount Zion. The action of Jesus is an assault on the existing form of the temple in general, a prophetic action that symbolically anticipates the demolition of the temple. From the Messiah one expected a reform of the cult (see Mal. 3:1–5; 1:11)—the cleansing of the temple is its prophetic-symbolic execution.

But what is it aiming at? What do the new cult and the new temple that Jesus seeks to achieve with his prophetic gesture look like? According to the Synoptic Gospels Jesus explained the meaning of this gesture with a saying that combines Isa. 56:7 and Jer. 7:11. In Isa. 56:7 we find the statement: "My house shall be called a house of prayer for all peoples." Here we must pay attention to the fact that the cleansing of the temple took place in the so-called *hieron*, the court of the Gentiles. Whereas only members of the chosen people could participate in the sacrificial worship of Israel in the temple court—the so-called *naos*—there was supposed to be room in the large court surrounding it for all peoples to pray with Israel to the God of the whole world. In the intervening period, however, this place of prayer had long since become a livestock market and an exchange bank; the cult of the law had crushed the broad reach of the words that called all human beings. In the false positivism of obedience to the law one had taken away the prayer space kept open for all the people. The cleansing of the temple is in fact a gesture of

opening the temple for all people; it is a prophetic anticipation of the promised pilgrimage of all people to the God of
Israel. In the explanation Jesus gives for his action, however,
God's words from Jer. 7:11 are also discernible: "Has this
house, which is called by my name, become a den of robbers
in your sight? You know, I too am watching, says the Lord."
This saying in Jeremiah was directed against that blind policy
which, in a foolish overestimation of its own strengths, did
not keep to the relationship of subjugation under Babylon
and risked war since it was thought that the Lord of heaven
and earth would defend his temple regardless of the circumstances. After all, he cannot be deprived either of his dwelling
place in the world or of his worship. God becomes a factor in
a foolish political calculation, and the temple becomes a "den
of robbers" in which the people imagine themselves to be safe
in an earthly fashion. This leads to the first destruction of the
temple and to the first dispersal of Israel. Jesus repeats Jeremiah's warning at a time when similar political ventures are
already clearly in the offing, and, like Jeremiah, he becomes a
martyr because he defends the true dwelling of God against
its earthly confiscation.

From this perspective we can now understand the puzzling
words Jesus speaks to the Jews in John's Gospel in response to
their question about the sign through which he shows his
authorization for reforming the cult: "Destroy (*lysate*) this temple, and in three days I will raise it up" (2:19). In a disguised
way Jesus is prophesying the end of the temple and with it the
end of the law, the end of the present form of the covenant. But
in a way that is no less mysterious he weaves his own fate into
this. The cleansing of the temple becomes a prophecy of his
death and a promise of his resurrection. Regardless of what its
precise formulation may have been, this saying was so bold and
so unprecedented that the first three Gospels did not dare to
recount it directly. They quote it only indirectly, on the lips of
the false witnesses at Jesus' trial and on the lips of those mock-
ing Jesus at the foot of the cross (Mark 14:58 and Matt. 26:61;

Mark 15:29 and Matt. 27:40). From this we know that the crime against the cult—the attack on the temple and thus on the very center of religion, the worship of God—played a major role in Jesus' martyrdom. The fact that the first martyr in the history of the Church, Stephen, was also killed because he had attacked the temple shows how sensitive this issue was. In this context it is also understandable why the Synoptics shied away from placing these words directly in the mouth of Jesus: that would have caused the failure of the attempt to unite all Israel in the faith in Jesus, an attempt that would still continue for a long time. The power of the words is weakened for the sake of peace. John, seeing that the separation has irreparably happened, is the first to come to the fore in an uninhibited way with the sharp clarity of the beginning. But what is actually being said here? It is prophesied that a living body that has gone through death will take the place of the stone temple. It is prophesied that the period of sacrifice according to the law is over and that he who is raised from the dead to new life takes its place. It is prophesied that he, the rejected stone, will become the cornerstone of God's new house. The crucified body of Jesus Christ who stretches his hands out over the whole world (cf. John 12:32) is the site where God and humans meet. The Risen One is the perpetual abiding of humans in God and of God in humans; he is the truth that replaces the images; he is the fount of the Spirit through whom worship in spirit and truth becomes possible. Through him God builds his house. If we look back from here to the starting point, the prophecy of Nathan, we can see that Jesus indeed does not destroy the Old Covenant, but only pushes aside that which has "come in in-between" and lays bare the core—fulfills the essence of the promise. But something else becomes clear as well: to be fitted into the new house as a living stone means to undergo the fate of the passion. The fate of the cornerstone reveals the plan of the entire building. One had to suffer and die for the break-through out of the narrowness of legal positivism and its national particularism. The new dimension will not be achieved without the passion of transformation. When describing the congregation or the Church as the new temple, as God's building, as God's house or as the body of Christ, early Christian preaching could draw its concepts from already existing rough drafts, for instance, from Qumran, which was also familiar with the designation temple for the congregation.[4] But only through the death of Jesus Christ did this insight acquire real meaning. From a spiritualized way of speaking it had become the most concentrated of all reality. The spiritual temple was no longer a spiritual cliché, but a reality paid for in body and blood whose vitality was able to permeate the centuries.

WHAT PROMPTED THE BUILDING OF CHRISTIAN CHURCHES?

But now it is time to ask: Does all this not stand in crass opposition to what we are doing here? After all, are we not honoring the stone building in which we are again trying to pull God into the world, as was done before?[5]

Since Constantine, have we not regressed into that interim period again, that in-between time which Christ overcame through his passion and resurrection? Has not the Church with the magnificence of her cathedrals strayed from the simplicity of Jesus and retreated down the path away from the direction in which Jesus pointed? Are we not passing off as Christian what in truth is a sign of its loss? Indeed, rather than celebrating the anniversary of a stone building, should we not be striding away from the fossilized past in a bold and resolute manner? Should we not instead be building a new community which worships God by taking care of human beings in a radical way? Did not that author point out the right path who quite consciously entitled his religious instruction *The House of Humans* in order to steer people away from the houses of God and to that house of humans whose construction would be a real imitation of Jesus? Even if we want to be less radical in our formulations, we must at least ask: What are we celebrating when we celebrate the millennium of a cathedral? How should we celebrate in order to remain on that path which leads from Nathan to the temple prophecy of Jesus, the rejected cornerstone?

Before we try to answer these questions it will be helpful to consider the following: What did the situation really look like in the emerging Church? What conclusions did the Church draw from the words and action of Jesus? How did it come about that by the time of Constantine's triumph a type of church construction was already fully developed? How did one perceive it? How were spirit and stone related to each other? There is scholarly research on all these questions whose results are very complex and also in part still very controversial. From these I would like to select just three basic themes:

1. Like Jesus himself, the apostles loved the temple as a place of prayer. From the Acts of the Apostles (3:1) we know that Peter and John went "up to the temple at the hour of prayer, at three o'clock in the afternoon," but of course not to take part in the afternoon Tamid offering "but because it is the hour at which the true Tamid and Passover sacrifice bleeds to death; with the community they praise the Father for this with an 'offering of the lips.'"[6] Continuity and discontinuity are visible here at one and the same time. Unlike the Qumran sect, the disciples of Jesus pray with Israel in her temple; they remain within the prayer community of God's covenant. But in contrast to the old and obsolete form of the law, they go to Solomon's Portico to pray without taking part in the sacrificial service. For them the temple is a house of prayer; they move in that part of the temple which may be described as a kind of synagogue—indeed as the starting point of synagogues in general.[7] The sacrificial cult was bound to Jerusalem, but the house of prayer could be everywhere. They kept that part of the temple which has a promising future: the place of congregation, the place of proclamation, the place of prayer. As a result, they did away

with the exclusivity of the temple on the one hand and preserved that which is universal and can be repeated everywhere on the other. The temple is thus fundamentally nothing
other than the synagogue, the space that brings people
together before the God of the covenant, the God of Jesus
Christ. It still has a special significance as the primordial cell
of all assembly, as a sign of the unity of God's history throughout the centuries, but wherever else an assembly occurs that is
essentially the same as in the temple, i.e., there is temple. Thus
all the exclusivity of this building had disappeared without
any disloyalty toward the history of faith expressed in the
Jerusalem shrine. It was understood to be the house of prayer
for all peoples; with that the precondition for the universality
of the Church was created at the same time.

Externally this shift is most obvious in the change of direction for prayer: no matter where they are, Jews pray facing
Jerusalem—the temple is the point of reference for all religion
so that the connection to God, the prayer relationship, always
has to go through the temple, even if only through the direction one faces at prayer. Christians pray not in the direction
of the temple but toward the east. The rising sun, which tri-
umphs over the night, symbolizes the risen Christ and is
simultaneously understood to be a sign of his Second Coming. Through their position at prayer Christians show that the
direction toward the Risen One is the true point of reference
of their life with God.[8] For this reason eastward orientation
has become the governing principle for Christian churches
over the centuries; it is an expression of the omnipresence of
the Lord's power to assemble, the Lord who reigns throughout the whole world like the rising sun. This shows clearly
that the emerging Church by no means rejects the room of
prayer, the place where people are gathered into the word and
into the transpired history of faith; it universalizes the temple
and thereby creates new possibilities for structuring it. Concentration on Solomon's Portico and opening up to the
expanse of the world do not spell the end of holy places. Just

the opposite is the case: since the living house, which is the issue here, is supposed to gather all human beings together, houses of assembly and places of prayer are now growing all over the world.

2. By the time Constantine promulgated his Edict of Tolerance for Christians, the church building had already found its definitive form. Eusebius recounts that the places that had been destroyed by the tyrant "rose anew from a long and deadly fall" and that "the churches rose up to immeasurable heights from scratch and became much more magnificent than the destroyed ones had been."[9] Previously the "jealous fiend . . . like a rabid dog" had turned "his brutish insanity first of all against the stones of our temples" and made "the churches into barren sites, or so he thought."[10] Thus, what happens under Constantine is reconstruction, not the transition from a religion of the spirit to a religion of stones. But we must ask: what idea had lent those early buildings their shape? What justifies them and brings them into harmony with the tradition of the origin? In the face of only very fragmentary traces of circumstantial evidence, these questions are being disputed up to the present moment and will probably always be disputed. The most plausible theory is the one that explains the earliest form of the Christian basilica from the theology of the martyrs.[11] In its essential design the basilica corresponds to the audience hall in which the god-emperor presented himself in a spectacle that was to be interpreted as the epiphany, the appearance of the divine. For the Christians this self-portrayal of the Caesar was a blasphemous event; over against the emperor's divine claim they placed the kingdom of God in the crucified and risen Christ. He alone was really that which the Caesars only claimed to be. Thus, the assembly room of Christians where the Lord continued to give himself to his own in the broken bread and the poured-out wine became the site of *their* cult of the emperor—the audience hall of the true king. For this antithesis they died;

martyrdom has been set into the design of this room, as it were. Following Solomon's Portico and the synagogue, one had first emphasized in a special way the promise from the sayings of Jesus that the house of prayer is for all peoples; but now the emphasis is on God's building a living house for himself through the passion of his own people and on his also taking the stones into his service precisely for this reason. This brings to light at the same time the motif that distinguishes the Christian ecclesia from the Jewish synagogue: its axis is not the Torah scroll but the living Lord; he builds it, and it is built in response to him. The christological factor through which the Church is more and other than the synagogue enters into the shape of the room, as it were, translating the inner essence of the Church into something visible.

3. In the course of history the motives and patterns are multiplied. There is no doubt that less valuable, remote, even negative aspects find their way in as well. Two basic ideas seem to me to dominate in a positive way. One is the motif of the incarnation. John has described Jesus' flesh as the tent of the Word (1:14).[12] The flesh of Jesus is the temple; it is the tent, the *shekinah*. For John the flesh of Jesus is paradoxically the truth and the spirit, which take the place of the old buildings. But now the idea awakens in Christianity that precisely God's incarnation was his entry into matter, the beginning of a momentous movement in which all matter is to become a vessel for the Word, but also in which the Word consistently has to make a statement about itself in matter, has to surrender itself to matter in order to be in a position to transform it. As a consequence, Christians are now deriving pleasure from making faith visible, from constructing its symbol in the world of matter. The other basic idea is connected to this: the idea of glorification, the attempt to turn the earth into praise, right down to the stones themselves, and thus to anticipate the world to come. The buildings in which faith is expressed

are, as it were, a visualized hope and a confident statement of what can come to be, projected into the present.

CONSEQUENCES FOR TODAY

After this discussion, let us now return to our questions from above: What is the relationship between the stone building and the building of living stones? Is it Christian to celebrate the building of a cathedral? If so, what are we celebrating when we do this? How should we celebrate so that we truly celebrate in a Christian way? I would like to respond in four steps.

1. The spirit builds the stones, not vice versa. The spirit cannot be replaced with money or with history. Where the spirit does not build, the stones become silent. Where the spirit is not alive, where it is not effective and does not reign, cathedrals become museums, memorials to the past whose beauty makes you sad because it is dead. That is the warning, as it were, which emanates from this cathedral celebration. Our history's greatness and our financial potency do not save us; both can turn into debris that smothers us. If the spirit does not build, money builds in vain. Faith alone can keep cathedrals alive, and the question the one-thousand-year-old cathedral is asking us is whether we have the strength of faith to give it a present and a future. In the end, organizations for the protection of historical monuments do not preserve the cathedral, as important and commendable as they are—only the spirit which created it can do this.

2. The spirit builds the stones, not vice versa—this also denotes the essential replaceability and the fundamental equivalence of all church buildings, whether we like it or not. Wherever people let the Lord gather them together, wherever he grants them his presence in Word and sacrament, there the

saying about the house of prayer being for all peoples is present; there the promise of the "upper room," the room of the Last Supper is fulfilled.[13] The hierarchical differences between the individual church buildings exist only on a second level, but they are for this reason by no means unimportant. Apart from the considerations of art history, a church building can receive a particular rank in principally two ways. It can first of all result from the history of faith and prayer that has taken root there. That we pray in the same churches in which our predecessors have been bringing their petitions and hopes before God over the centuries is not irrelevant. In St. Ludger's Church in Münster it has always moved me deeply to know that this was the place where Edith Stein struggled with her vocation. And this is just a tiny excerpt from the history of faith and prayer and the history of sinners and saints preserved in our great old churches. Thus they are also an expression of the identity of faith throughout history, an expression of the faithfulness of God which reveals itself in the unity of the Church. Or should it not move us to know that a thousand years ago the bishop of Mainz spoke the same words of consecration and used basically the same missal in his cathedral as his successors today? The other thing that can distinguish a church building is its position in the organization of the living assembly that is the Church. The special rank of the bishop's church is derived from this; it directs our attention to the bishop as the focus of the Church community. The cathedral expresses in stone that the Church is not an amorphous mass of parishes but exists in an interconnection that binds each individual parish beyond its own borders to the whole through the cohesion of the episcopal system. For this very reason the Second Vatican Council, which called to mind the episcopal organization of the Church with such vigor, also quite emphatically stressed the rank of the cathedral church. The individual churches refer to it—are built around it, so to speak—and precisely in this cohesion and in this organization individual churches effect the assembly and oneness of the Church. For the same reason the cathedral churches of the common bishop of all Christianity, the Lateran and St. Peter's in Rome, mean a great deal to us. Not as if God were more present there than in any village church, but because they express the assembly and the uniqueness of God's house in the many places of worship on earth. If one would reject this connection and negate this visible ordering of the churches to each other, one would be renouncing precisely the promise that the house of prayer is for *all* peoples. This promise is fulfilled in particular when the apostolic ordering of the assembly is reflected in the classification of the places of assembly which thus become one single house.

3. This signifies the basic openness of all places of worship which are either a part of the whole Church or are not really Church at all. In order to maintain its Christian legitimacy the church building must be "catholic" in the original sense of the word: home of the faithful everywhere. A number of years ago a book of pictures was published with the title *You Are at Home Everywhere*. These words articulate in fact a task for the Church which began her journey under the dictum that the house of prayer is for all peoples. In one of his early works describing a trip to Prague, Albert Camus writes in a distressing way about the experience of being in a foreign place, of being isolated. In a city whose language he does not understand he is like an exile; even the magnificence of the churches remains silent and offers no comfort.[14] For those who believe, it should not be possible for this to happen: where there is Church, where there is the eucharistic presence of the Lord, they experience home. But before this can occur, something just the opposite of this is required: faith must be experienced as assembly, as oneness; people entering the realm of faith must leave behind what is merely their own and let catholicity, the turning of themselves over to the whole, happen to them as an ongoing process. In the face of the *Zeit-*

geist and the many forms of chauvinism, it is imperative that the faithful take upon themselves the condition of being foreign, which is necessary so that there be a home for the whole in all places, so that the same home, as it were, is encountered everywhere. This again raises questions for us: How does this actually work? Can legal immigrants find a home in our churches? Can foreigners find people there who understand them? When viewed correctly, this transcending of what is one's own which is under discussion here definitely has something to do with the theology of passion found at the start of the Christian way. Only those who have set out on the path to become free of themselves, only those who have taken at least a few steps can meet foreigners and offer them a home. The Church Fathers were acquainted with the beautiful metaphor that the stones have to be hewn and matched to become a building and that people who are to become one house are not spared this either.

4. Let us once again return to the fundamental question about spirit and stone, about the living house and the stone church. The direction in which Christ's words point and in which the early Church continues to go can with good reason be described as "spiritualization." But if it were only that, then Christianity would not stand out from a trend that we come across in the entire Mediterranean region at the time of Jesus, in Judaism as well as in the Hellenistic world. The particularity of the Christian way consists of the fact that the Christian spiritualization is simultaneously an incarnation.[15] Paul has splendidly formulated its motto: "Now the Lord is the Spirit" (2 Cor. 3:17). This distinguishes it from all other kinds of spiritualization, whether philosophical or merely mystical. The Spirit into which it transforms all that has come to pass is the body of Christ. Accordingly, an authentic development of the Christian beginning has to turn against a vapid sort of spiritualizing propaganda that seeks the spirit without the body and thereby destroys the spirit as well. The opposite

misunderstanding must of course also be rejected which sees in the word "incarnation" the justification for every kind of secularization as well as an institutional ossification of the faith. During the golden age of incarnational theology one liked to say that the things of the earth had to be baptized. All right, but one must not forget that baptism is a sacrament of death, that we are baptized into the death of Christ, that to be baptized means to go through or rather to go into the transformation of death in order to move toward the risen Christ. To spiritualize means to incarnate in a Christian way, but to incarnate means to spiritualize, to bring the things of the world to the coming Christ, to prepare them for their future form and thus to prepare God's future in the world. In St. Irenaeus's work we find the lovely thought that the meaning of the incarnation was for the Spirit—the Holy Spirit—to get used to the flesh, as it were, in Jesus.[16] Turning this around we could say: The meaning of ongoing incarnation can only be the reverse, to get the flesh used to the Spirit, to God, to make it *capax spiritus* and in this way to prepare its future.

But what does all this mean in terms of our question? Well, to begin with, I think it takes us back to what is completely elementary which is fundamental for all New Testament statements, namely, that in fact God himself first builds his house, or, to express it in a more accessible way for us, that we cannot do it alone, on our own. Such a statement is directed against those who believe that with a certain number of walled-in square meters the task is done as well as against those who want to create the Church anew in a chemically pure way in the retort of their pastoral strategies. God builds his house; that is, it does not take shape where people only want to plan, achieve, and produce by themselves. It does not appear where only success counts and where all the "strategies" are measured by success. It does not materialize where people are not prepared to make space and time in their lives for him; it does not get constructed where people only build by themselves and for themselves. But where people let themselves be claimed for God, there they have time for him and there space is available for him. There they can dare to represent in the present what is to come: the dwelling of God with us and our gathering together through him, which make us sisters and brothers of one house. Being open to simplicity is just as natural here as recognizing the right to beauty, to the beautiful. Indeed, the beautiful only becomes evident in its transforming and comforting power in such spiritualization of the world toward the coming Christ. Something unusual is revealed here as well: the house of God is the true house of humans. It becomes the house of humans even more the less it tries to be this and the more it is simply put up for him. We only have to think for a moment what Europe would really look like if we took all the churches away from it. It would be a desert of utility in which the heart would probably stop beating. Where people just want to inhabit the earth by themselves it becomes uninhabitable. Nothing more is built up where humans only want to build by themselves and for themselves. But where they pull back and part with their time and their space, there the house of the community is built, there a piece of utopia, of the impossible on earth, becomes a present reality. The beauty of the cathedral does not stand in opposition to the theology of the cross, but is its fruit: it was born from the willingness not to build one's city by oneself and for oneself. The misuse of something just for oneself is of course not excluded by this. No church building possesses the promise of eternity; none is irreplaceable; each can be taken from us when the power justifying it crumbles.

"Built from living stones"—if there had not been living stones at the beginning, these stones would not be standing here. Now, however, they speak to us. They call upon us to build the living cathedral, to be the living cathedral so that the cathedral of stone remains a present reality and heralds the future.

Notes

1. For the exegesis, see K. H. Schelkle, *Die Petrusbriefe, Der Judasbrief* (Freiburg, 1961), pp. 57–63; the following are also recommended from the wealth of literature available: J. Coppens, "Le sacerdoce royal des fidèles: un commentaire de I Petri II, 4–10," in *Au service de la parole de Dieu: Mélanges offerts à Mgr. A. M. Charue* (Gembloux, 1969), pp. 61–75; J. H. Elliott, *The Elect and the Holy: An Exegetical Examination of 1 Peter 2, 4–10* (Leiden, 1966). On the parallel text, Eph. 2:19–22, see J. Gnilka, *Der Epheserbrief* (Freiburg, 1971), pp. 152–60; on the stone motif in the New Testament in general, see J. Betz, "Christus-Petra-Petrus," in *Kirche und Überlieferung*, ed. J. Betz and H. Fries (Freiburg, 1960), pp. 1–21.

2. On the problem of interpreting the text of 2 Sam. 7:1–29, see H. W. Hertzberg, *Die Samuelbücher*, 3rd ed. (Göttingen, 1965). On the entire complex of the theology of the temple, see Y. Congar, *Le mystère du temple* (Paris, 1957).

3. On the theme of Jesus and the temple, see Y. Congar, *Le mystère*, pp. 133–80, as well as the substantial material in R. Bultmann, *Das Evangelium des Johannes* (Göttingen, 1957), pp. 85–91; and R. Schnackenburg, *Das Johannesevangelium* (Freiburg, 1965), 1:359–71 [Eng.: *The Gospel according to St. John* (New York, 1980)]. The reader will readily note that in what follows I am not trying to enter into the debate about the *ipsissima facta et verba* of Jesus, but simply trying to describe the Jesus of the Gospels—certainly a worthwhile and largely neglected undertaking after so many depictions of the "historical Jesus."

4. See R. Schnackenburg, *Das Johannesevangelium*, 1:365. The ideas touched on here concerning the unity of the Testaments and the "must" of the passion I tried to expand and explain further in a lecture on Israel, the Church, and the world given in Jerusalem in 1994; it has been published in my little book *Evangelium, Katechese und Katechismus* (Munich, 1995), pp. 63–83.

5. This essay was written as a speech for the celebration of the millennium of the Cathedral of Mainz.

6. F. Mussner, "Die UNA SANCTA nach Apg 2,42," in idem, *Praesentia salutis: Gesammelte Studien zu Fragen und Themen des Neuen Testaments* (Düsseldorf, 1967), pp. 212–22 (quotation from p. 221).

7. Ibid., pp. 220–21.

8. E. Peterson, "Die geschichtliche Bedeutung der jüdischen Gebetsrichtung," in idem, *Frühkirche, Judentum und Gnosis: Studien und Untersuchungen* (Freiburg, 1959), pp. 1–14.

9. Eusebius, *Hist. Eccl.* 10.2; I am following Ph. Haeuser's translation (Kempten, 1932) in the new edition by H. Kraft (Munich, 1967), p. 412 [translated into English from the German].

10. Ibid., 10.14; quoted in Kraft, p. 416 [translated into English from the German].

11. See B. Kötting, "Die Gestaltung des Kultraumes in der frühen Kirche," in idem, *Ecclesia peregrinans* (Münster, 1988), 2:186–98. Recent clarifications concerning the essence and development of the Christian church can be found in the important little book by L. Bouyer, *Architecture et liturgie* (Paris, 1991).

12. Furthermore, it is probably not irrelevant that the word *shekinah* was discernible in the Greek word *skēnē* and thus it identified Jesus as the place of God's presence; see Bultmann, *Das Evangelium des Johannes* (see n. 3), p. 43; Schnackenburg, *Das Johannesevangelium* (see n. 3), p. 245; *Theological Dictionary of the New Testament*, 7:378–79; Haag, *Bibellexikon*, 1536.

13. With this remark I would like to suggest that in addition to Solomon's Portico the room of the Last Supper and of the Pentecost event must be seen as a second early Christian precursor of the church building. Only half of the Christian religious service, the Liturgy of the Word, transpires in Solomon's Portico. The feature most interiorly proper to and characteristic of the new community, the Lord's Supper, which replaces and fulfills the old sacrifices, cannot find space there. Only when the cenacle and Solomon's Portico come together in one room is "church" realized in the specific sense. If you overlook this, you not only arrive at a purely "synagogal" construction of the church building, but of Christianity as a whole and so miss the central point in the end.

14. A. Camus, "L'envers et l'endroit: La mort dans l'âme," in idem, *Essais* (Bibl. de la Pléiade, 1965), pp. 31–39. Cf. G. Linde, *Das Problem der Gottesvorstellungen im Werk von Albert Camus* (Münster, 1975), especially pp. 10–11.

15. I tried to describe the problem of spiritualization and incarnation in somewhat more detail in the essay "On the Theological Basis of Church Music" in my book *The Feast of Faith*, trans. Graham Harrison (San Francisco: Ignatius Press, 1986), pp. 97–126; see also the relevant essays of this volume.

16. *Adversus Haereses* 5.12.4, *Sources chrétiennes* 153, 154. See also H. J. Jaschke, *Der Heilige Geist im Bekenntnis der Kirche: Ein Studie zur Pneumatologie des Irenaeus von Lyon im Ausgang vom altchristlichen Glaubensbekenntnis* (Münster, 1976).

6

"Sing Artistically for God":
Biblical Directives for
Church Music

❧

PRELIMINARY REMARKS ON THE SITUATION
OF CHURCH AND CULTURE

Since church music is faith that has become a form of culture, it necessarily shares in the current problematic nature of the relationship between Church and culture. In this relationship there are problems on both sides. The inner connection of faith to culture is in the throes of a crisis. Since the end of the Enlightenment, faith and contemporary culture have drifted apart more and more. Up to that time culture had developed from the roots of religion in Christian Europe, as in all history, and had remained tied to this matrix even in its secular forms of expression. The Renaissance and the Reformation marked a first crisis for this blending of Church and culture. But not until the Enlightenment does a real cultural revolution, a decisive emancipation of culture from faith occur. The two go

119

their separate ways, even if the nineteenth century was still marked by a lively exchange between them. In any case, whoever looks at a number of neo-gothic or neo-romanesque churches sees that the Church, although she was not able to disavow her epoch, was still being pushed back into a kind of subculture that was marginalized on the edge of the mainstream of cultural development. This situation is also apparent in the relationship between the Caecilian reform of church music and the general development of music during the second half of the nineteenth century as well as at the beginning of the twentieth century. It should not be denied, however, that within this "subcultural" movement great things were accomplished that can be placed beside the main trend in culture at that time since they are of completely equal rank. It should not be denied that the historicizing tendency visible in the renewal of older styles and in the connection of faith to the cultural expression of earlier periods also corresponded to the spirit of the century. Finally we should not forget that such an important cultural event as the rediscovery and renewal of Gregorian chant and great polyphonic church music was the fruit of such orientations, which have thus displayed a significant intellectual productivity. But all in all the gap has become wider and wider, and in the confusing conflict between the cultural experiments and cultureless pragmatic activities of the Church today it is obvious that we are at a loss as to how faith can and should express itself culturally in the present age.

Even for modern culture, however, the separation from its religious matrix has not been without consequences. For this reason it, too, has been driven into a dead end in which it can say less and less about its own *quo vadis*. Culture somehow seems useless in the modern world and, making a virtue out of necessity, it defines itself frankly as follows: Art is that which fulfills no function but is simply just there. There is some truth to this, but negation alone does not suffice to establish a meaningful space for any kind of phenomenon in the existential framework of humans and the world. The difficulties that art has gotten into through the complete secularization of culture are becoming particularly clear in the area of music. Like any other cultural expression, music always had different levels, from the unsophisticated singing of simple people, which is nevertheless genuine in itself, to the highest artistic perfection. But now something completely new has occurred. Music has split into two worlds that hardly have anything to do with each other any more. On the one hand there is the music of the masses, which, with the label "pop" or popular music, would like to portray itself as the music of the people. Here music has become a product that can be industrially manufactured and is evaluated by how well it sells. On the other hand there is a rationally construed, artificial music with the highest technical requirements which is hardly capable of reaching out beyond a small, elite circle. In the middle between the two extremes we find the recourse to history, a staying at home in the familiar music that preceded such divisions, touched the person as a whole and is still capable of doing this even today. It is understandable that church music mostly settles in this middle ground. But since the Church, after all, is living in this age it was inevitable that she also try her hand at the two opposing spheres of today's cultural schizophrenia. When people rightly call for a new dialogue between Church and culture today, they must not forget in the process that this dialogue must necessarily be bilateral. It cannot consist in the Church finally subjecting herself to modern culture, which has been caught up to a large extent in a process of self-doubt since it lost its religious base. Just as the Church must expose herself to the problems of our age in a radically new way, so too must culture be questioned anew about its groundlessness and its ground, and in the process be opened to a painful cure, that is, to a new reconciliation with religion since it can get its lifeblood only from there.

For this reason the issue of church music is really a very vital piece of a comprehensive task for our age which requires more than mere dialogue; it requires a process of rediscovering ourselves. When theologians try to contribute something in this struggle, they must make use of the means available to them. They cannot enter into the musical discussions per se, but they can nonetheless ask where the seams are, so to speak, that link faith and art. They can try to explain how faith prepares an interior place for art and which directives it gives for the path of art. This, too, would still be a very extensive undertaking if one wanted to explore the entire range of available theological sources. All the sources, however, ultimately depend on the original source, on the Bible; I would therefore like to limit myself to the question whether there are biblical directives for the path of church music. Because of the extent and complexity of the biblical witness it is necessary to narrow this down once more. I am asking concretely: Can we find one biblical text that sums up the way Holy Scripture sees the connection between music and faith?

A Psalm Verse as Mirror of the Biblical Directives for Music in Worship

A first approach to the topic presents itself if we recall that the Bible contains its own hymnal: the Psalter, which was not only born from the practice of singing and playing musical instruments during worship but also contains by itself—in the practice, the live performance—essential elements of a theory of music in faith and for faith. We must pay attention to the place of this book in the biblical canon in order to appreciate its significance properly. Within the Old Testament the Psalter is a bridge, as it were, between the Law and the Prophets. It has grown out of the requirements of the temple cult, of the law, but by appropriating the law in prayer and song it has uncovered its prophetic essence more and more. It has led beyond the ritual and its ordinances into the "offering of praise," the "wordly offering" with which people open themselves to the Logos and thus become worship with him. In this way the Psalter has also become a bridge connecting the two Testaments. In the Old Testament its hymns had been considered to be the songs of David; this meant for Christians that these hymns had risen from the heart of the real David, Christ. In the early church the psalms are prayed and sung as hymns to Christ. Christ himself thus becomes the choir director who teaches us the new song and gives the Church the tone and the way in which she can praise God appropriately and blend into the heavenly liturgy.

As a main connecting theme for my comments I would like to select one verse from the Psalter which appears again and again in the history of theological reflection on the foundations and path of church music, and this with justification since it mirrors something of the basic orientation of the book of Psalms as a whole. I am referring to the seventh verse of Psalm 47 [in some Bibles the eighth verse and/or Psalm 46; NRSV 47:8]. The ecumenical Bible for German-speaking countries translates this verse in a rather vacuous way: Sing a psalm [*Singt ein Psalmenlied*]. It leaves it up to the one reading or praying to imagine what this—"a psalm"—could be. In contrast M. Buber and F. Rosenzweig had translated it: "Play as an inspiration" [*Eine Eingebungsweise spielt auf*]. They are emphasizing the artistic inspiration that should stand behind the requested song. A more distinctive interpretation of the word in question, "psalm," is offered by A. Deissler, who translates it as "artistic hymn."[1] In his outstanding commentary on the psalms, H.-J. Kraus comes to a similar decision, for he writes: "Sing an art song."[2] The [French] translation of the Jerusalem Bible is along the same lines: "Play for God with all your art [with all your skill]."[3] The translation issued by the Italian Bishops' Conference also speaks of singing "con arte" (artistically). That more or less covers the spectrum of the attempts to approximate the Hebrew expression *maśkîl* in modern translations. But the old translations that reflect the efforts of the early Church are also important for us. The

Septuagint, which became the Old Testament of Christianity, wrote *psalate synetōs,* which we might translate as: "Sing in an understandable way; sing with understanding"—in both senses of the word: that you yourselves understand it and that it is understandable. Of course there is more to this expression than our rationalistic idea of understanding and understandability: Sing from and toward the spirit; sing in a way worthy of and appropriate to the spirit, disciplined and pure. The translation that Jerome chose and which was taken up again in the Sixto-Clementine Vulgate is along the same lines: *psallite sapienter.* Singing psalms should have something of the essence of *sapientia* about it and in it. In order to plumb the enigmatic quality of this formulation we should ponder what is meant by *sapientia*: a behavior of humans that certainly has the brilliance of understanding about it but also denotes an integration of the entire human person who not only understands and is understandable from the perspective of pure thought, but with all the dimensions of his or her existence. In this respect there is an affinity between wisdom and music, since in it such an integration of humanness occurs and the entire person becomes a being in accordance with logos [with "reason"]. Finally we should also note that in the similar context of Psalm 33 (32):3 the Vulgate is acquainted with the expression "play the psalms well" or "sing well" (*bene cantare*), which Augustine, for example, quite naturally interprets as singing in the way the *ars musicae* teaches.[4] Thus, from the verse of a psalm, the Church became aware of the need for an artistic level of musical expression in the praise of God.

With these comments we have tried first of all to delineate the literal meaning of the biblical text and its reception in the Church. Now we have to ask: What follows for liturgical music from this biblical imperative and which conclusions were attached to it in the emerging Church? In such an analysis, which of course cannot go into scholarly details, two words in our psalm verse must be considered carefully; they

are both momentous and have therefore been—and remain—
laden with history. To begin with, there is the first word,
which in German is translated somewhat innocuously as
"sing." On the path from the Hebrew word *zāmîr* to the
Greek phrasing *psalate*, however, a cultural and intellectual
development had already occurred that had a determining
influence on the entire history to come and which still has
something very concrete to say to us as well. Just the choice of
the Hebrew word already presupposes a cultural decision-
making process that is based on a religious orientation and
marks the peculiarity of Israel in the history of the religions of
the Near East as well as of humanity in general. The word
zāmîr is based on a stem found in all old Hamito-Semitic languages. The word means singing with or without instrumental
accompaniment; the emphasis is on articulated singing, a
singing with reference to a text, which is instrumentally supported as a rule but always ordered to a specific statement in
regard to content.[5] Thus, *zāmîr* stands clearly apart from
orgiastic cult music, which serves to intoxicate the senses and
which, through the frenzy of sensual feelings, carries people
away in the ecstatic "liberation" from mind and will. In contrast, *zāmîr* refers to logos-like music, if we can put it that
way, which incorporates a word or wordlike event it has
received and responds to it in praise or petition, in thanksgiving or lament. The Septuagint chose the word *psallein* in its
translation, which for the Greeks meant "to touch, pluck, run
with the fingers, particularly when playing strings," in general
to play a stringed instrument, but never to sing.[6] The Greek
Bible gave the Greek word a completely new meaning, and
with that it also introduced a cultural change. Although the
word *psalmos* had denoted a stringed instrument in Greek, it
now meant the songs of Israel which arise from faith. The verb
likewise acquired the meaning "to sing," but now in a sense
that is quite clearly defined by the history of a civilization and
religion: to sing as Israel sings to her God. In this sense the
expression "to sing psalms" is a neologism of the Bible with

which it also introduced a new phenomenon into the Greek world. It denotes a singing that found its clearly defined musical form in the prayer tradition of Israel; Martin Hengel describes this form as follows: "Since the number of syllables per line of verse was not fixed, it is not a matter of singing a thoroughly composed melody, but of a . . . sprechgesang which probably only permitted melody-like movements of tone at the beginning and the end of the stichs."[7]

The analysis of the oft-repeated imperative *psallite* in the psalms thus allows us to draw a few concrete conclusions concerning our question about possible biblical directives for music in the Church:

1. This imperative runs through all of Scripture; it is the concrete version of the call to worship and glorify God which is revealed in the Bible as the most profound vocation of human beings. This means that musical expression is part of the proper human response to God's self-revelation, to his becoming open to a relationship with us. Mere speech, mere silence, mere action are not enough. That integral way of humanly expressing joy or sorrow, consent or complaint which occurs in singing is necessary for responding to God, who touches us precisely in the totality of our being. In the course of this discussion we have seen that the word *psallite* entails more than our word "to sing"; it does not necessarily require instrumental accompaniment, but because of its origin it does refer to instruments in which, as it were, creation is made to sound. Admittedly the biblical adaptation of this word has made singing—that is, making music vocally— primary.[8]

2. The musical imperative of the Bible is therefore not entirely unspecified but refers to a form that biblical faith gradually created for itself as the appropriate mode of its expression. There is no such thing as a faith completely undetermined by culture, so to speak, which would then let itself be inculturated any way one likes. The faith decision as such

entails a cultural decision; it forms the people, and by doing this it excludes a good many other cultural patterns as deformations. Faith itself creates culture and does not just carry it along like a piece of clothing added from the outside. This cultural given, which cannot be manipulated as one likes and which determines the extent of all subsequent inculturations, is neither rigid nor closed in on itself. The level of a culture is discernible by its ability to assimilate, to come into contact and exchange, and to do this synchronically and diachronically. It is capable of encountering other contemporary cultures as well as the development of human culture in the march of time. This ability to exchange and flourish also finds its expression in the ever-recurring imperative: "Sing the Lord a new song." Experiences of salvation are found not only in the past, but occur over and over again; hence they also require the ever-new proclamation of God's contemporaneity, whose eternity is falsely understood if one interprets it as being locked in decisions made "from time immemorial." On the contrary, to be eternal means to be synchronous with all times and to be ahead of all times.

The summons to sing a new song acquired a very special meaning for Christians. They saw it as the command to pass from the Old to the New Covenant, to transpose the psalms in a christological fashion. Particularly in the Toda-psalms one finds a type of prayer that grew out of the faith of Israel; this prayer, deep down inside, was on the path into the newness of the New Covenant.[9] The following characteristics belong to the schema of these psalms: asking for help in dire need, experiencing banishment into the abyss of death, vowing to proclaim God's great deed if one is saved, and keeping this vow by singing of God's favor before the congregation so as to give thanks and bring humans the message of God's gracious power. This schema had been expanded into a new song time and again from the viewpoint of the various verifications of salvation. But the truly new, which had hitherto been merely awaited, happened only now, in the mystery of Jesus

Christ. The "new song" praises his death and resurrection and hence proclaims God's new deed to the whole world: that he himself has descended into the anguish of the human state and into the pit of death; that he embraces all of us on the cross with his stretched-out arms and, as the Risen One, takes us up to the Father across the abyss of the infinite divide separating creator and creature, which only crucified love can cross. Thus, the old song has become new and must be sung as such over and over again. In this process of renewal, however, the song has not done away with the basic cultural decision of faith nor with that which faith has culturally given as a directive but has opened them on the one hand even further while simultaneously defining them more clearly. The first centuries of Christianity confront us with a dramatic struggle for the right determination of the relationship between this openness of the new on the one hand and the irrevocable and fundamental cultural form on the other, which belongs to the essence of faith itself. This struggle must have been all the more provocative seeing that the transition worked by God from the old to the new song, from the prophetic to the christological version of the psalms, coincided with the historical transition from Semitic to Greek culture, so that in the cultural shift it was necessary to grapple very concretely with the questions of what was not relinquishable and of the possibility of a new form. Martin Hengel has shown how closely this cultural struggle was linked to the development of Christology itself, indeed, virtually coincided with it. We will have to come back to this, but for the moment we still have to complete our analysis of the psalm verse.[10]

3. We have already tried to probe the meaning of the second word in our psalm verse. We saw its range essentially delineated in the two translations *sapienter* and *cum arte*. It turned out that the meaning of *sapienter* leads in the same direction as the development in meaning given by the Greek Old Testament to the verb *psallein*. Speaking about singing in

accordance with wisdom points to a word-oriented art, but the place of word must not be narrowed in the superficially rationalistic sense of an intelligibility of all words at all times. Instead, looking at it from the perspective of the early Church, we can call what is meant here music in accordance with logos [with "reason"]. There is an art form corresponding to God, who, from the beginning and in each life, is the creative Word which also gives meaning. This art form stands under the primacy of logos; that is, it integrates the diversity of the human being from the perspective of this being's highest moral and spiritual powers, but in this way it also leads the spirit out of rationalistic and voluntaristic confinement into the symphony of creation.

The second translation, *cum arte*, told us that encountering God challenges a person's highest abilities. Humans can only correspond to God's greatness if they also give to their response, according to the extent of their ability, the complete dignity of the beautiful, the height of true "art." In this context we should recall the theory of art that the book of Exodus develops in connection with the construction of the sacred tabernacle.[11] Three elements are essential here. The artists themselves do not plan what might be worthy of God and beautiful. Humans are not capable of inventing this on their own. It is rather God himself who discloses to Moses the shape of the shrine, right down to the details. Artistic creation reproduces what God has shown as model. It presupposes the inner view of the exemplar; it is the conversion of a vision into form. Artistic creativeness as the Old Testament sees it is something completely different from what the modern age understands by creativity. Today creativity is understood to be the making of something that no one has made or thought of before, the invention of something that is completely one's own and completely new. In comparison with this, artistic creativeness in the book of Exodus is seeing together with God, participating in his creativity; it is exposing the beauty that is already waiting and concealed in creation. This does not diminish the worth of the artist, but is in fact its justification. For this reason it is also said that the Lord "has called by name" Bezalel, the principal artist for the construction of the sacred tabernacle (Exod. 35:30): the same set phrase or formula is valid for the artist as well as for the prophet. Furthermore, artists are described as people to whom the Lord has given understanding and skill so that they can carry out what God has instructed them to do (36:1). Finally, the fact that every artist's "heart was stirred" (36:2) belongs here as a third component. As far as I can see, what Exodus says about the fine arts is in fact not explicitly applied to liturgical music anywhere in the Bible.[12] But the mere fact that the Psalter as a whole was ultimately dedicated to King David entails an analogous evaluation: David is the king who has given God his dwelling place in Israel, on the holy mountain; he is the new founder of the cult, and he has become this precisely by showing the Holy People the way in which they can praise God with dignity. For church music this means that everything the Old Testament has to say about art—its necessity, its essence, and its dignity—is concealed in the *bene cantare* of the psalms.

ON THE ADOPTION OF THE BIBLICAL DIRECTIVES IN THE LITURGICAL LIFE OF THE CHURCH

We have thus returned to the question of the adoption of all this in the New Testament and consequently of the lasting significance of these biblical directives for the music of the Church. We had already seen that the Church regarded Christ, the true David, also as the true author of the psalms, and for this reason the Church embraced with a new hermeneutics the prayer- and hymnbook of the Old Covenant as her primary book for worship. With the text she adopted the mode of singing, that is, that basic cultural decision which had occurred during the development of the psalmody. She saw in it the standard that served as orientation for any new singing of the new song. This is quite apparent in the organization of worship found in the First Letter to the Corinthians: "When you come together, each one has a song (*psalmon*), a lesson, a revelation, a tongue, or an interpretation. Let all things be done for building up" (14:26). At the beginning of the service there is the song which Paul describes with the word "psalm" and thus defines in its musical and theological form.[13] For the assessment of art in the apostolic Church it is important that the song appeared as a gift of the Spirit just like the lesson, tongue, prophecy, and interpretation. From Pliny we learn that the sung glorification of Christ in his divinity belonged to the core of the Christian religious service at the beginning of the second century, and we may consider the prologue of John and the hymn in Philippians as archetypes of such songs.[14] The early development of Christology, its ever-deeper recognition of Christ's divinity, probably occurred essentially and particularly in the hymns of the Church, in the blend of theology, poetry, and music.

At this point, though, a delaying factor set in that is of great significance for our reflections. To the extent that it distanced itself from the Semitic world, the development of christological art songs threatened more and more to turn into an acute hellenization of Christianity, that is, to alienate itself from Christianity's own nature as culture and faith. The fascination of Greek music and Greek thinking led out of the faith by way of music so that the new music rapidly became the domain of Gnosticism—indeed, new music and gnosis virtually coalesced. For this reason the Church immediately and rigorously rejected the poetical and musical innovation and reduced church music to the Psalter in two senses: that the theology of the Psalter sufficed and set the standard in terms of content, but also in the sense that the way of making music specified by the Psalter became the musical model of emerging Christendom. This limitation of liturgical singing, which gradually began asserting itself from the second century, received its canonical expression in canon 59 of the Synod of Laodicea (364), which forbade the use of "private psalm compositions and non-canonical writings" in religious services. In addition, in canon 15 the singing of the Psalms is restricted to the choir, "whereas others should not sing in church." Somewhat later the so-called *Apostolic Constitutions* spoke in a similar way.[15] We can perhaps regret this phase of temporary restriction and lament the loss that occurred as a result of eradicating early Christian poetry. Nonetheless, this action was—historically speaking—essential for strengthening the Church's own cultural identity and, along with this, her identity in faith. Only in this way could she become a new source of cultural creativity, which began with renewed vigor in Alexandria already in the third century and then gave us the whole magnificent cultural inspiration that radiated from Christian faith in all the following centuries. Particularly in the area of music, the faith of the Church has become creative far beyond all other cultural spheres, not least of all because, in terms of its creative expression, it has constantly judged itself on the biblical directives and with the passage of time has learned to plumb their inner wealth. Without diminishing its promising future, sung prayer has unfolded and concretized this standard above all in three basic forms: Gregorian chant, the great polyphonic music of the early modern age, and church hymns.

CONSEQUENCES FOR TODAY

At the close there remains the question: What does all this mean for the present situation of faith and art? No one can answer this question in every detail at the moment. We only have approaches in which we must gradually try to learn to differentiate the right path from the wrong path in order to be of service to the daily practice of liturgical life on the one hand, yet also show the sphere where lively development can productively flourish on the other. At the outset we began with the modern art scene's schizophrenia between "pop" or popular music and elitist aestheticism. The two limits for church music have therefore already been indicated: if music crosses these boundaries, it sacrifices the culture of faith and hence stops being music from the word of God and for the word of God.

Against Aestheticism as an End in Itself

First of all, that hybrid aestheticism which excludes every function of art as service, that is, which can only regard art as having its own purpose and its own standard, is incompatible with the directives of the Bible. Wherever it is exhibited consistently this presumptuousness necessarily leads to a nihilistic lack of standards and therefore generates nihilistic parodies of art, but not a new creativity. The philosophy at work here belies the creaturely determination of the human being; it would like to elevate the human person to the level of a pure creator. But in this way it leads the human person into untruth, into contradiction with his or her own nature; untruth, however, always drifts into the disintegration of what is creative. Earlier we had briefly touched on the problematic nature of the modern concept of creativity in which the anthropological problem of the modern age is present in a concentrated way. In idealistic philosophy the human spirit is no longer primarily receptive—it does not receive, but is only productive.[16] In the existential radicalization of this approach, nothing meaningful at all precedes human existence. The human being comes from a meaningless factuality and is thrown into a meaningless freedom. The person thus becomes a pure creator; at the same time his or her creativity becomes a mere whim and, precisely for this reason, empty. According to Christian faith, however, it belongs to the essence of human beings that they come from God's "art," that they themselves are a part of God's art and as perceivers

can think and view God's creative ideas with him and translate them into the visible and the audible. If this be the case,
then to serve is not foreign to art; only by serving the Most
High does it exist at all. Music does not become alienated
from its own purpose when it praises God and praises him in
such a way that it becomes "proclamation in the great congregation" (Ps. 22:25). On the contrary, only from this willingness does it renew itself again and again. It is precisely the
test of true creativity that the artist steps out of the esoteric
circle and knows how to form his or her intuition in such a
way that the others—the many—may perceive what the artist
has perceived. In the process, the three conditions for true art
specified in the book of Exodus are always valid: artists must
be moved by their hearts; they must have understanding, that
is, be skillful people; and they must have perceived what the
Lord himself has shown.

Against Pastoral Pragmatism
as an End in Itself

Just like aesthetic elitism, pastoral pragmatism, which is only
looking for success, is also incompatible with the mission of
church music. When, in an earlier lecture entitled "Liturgy
and Church Music," I referred in this context to the incom-
patibility between rock and pop music and the liturgy of the
Church,[17] there quickly arose a loud cry of protest from those
who felt obliged to show once again their progressive cast of
mind. I heard very little of actual arguments in these protests.
My comments, though, were basically directed at rock music,
whose radical anthropological opposition to both faith's
image of human beings and its cultural intent has been amply
and competently elucidated by others.[18] I touched on pop
music only in passing, and so, as a matter of fact, one could
argue that my comments were not justified. Pop music, as we
have already said, wants to be popular music—"folk music"
in contrast to elitist art music. For this reason we can under-

stand the following questions: Is pop music not exactly what we need? Has the Church not always been the home of folk music? Has the high quality of the Church's musical expression not renewed itself again and again from the matrix of folk music?

Here we have to tread carefully. The audience to whom pop music refers is mass society. In contrast, folk music in its original sense is the musical expression of a clearly defined community held together by its language, history, and way of life, which assimilates and shapes its experiences in song—the experience with God, the experiences of love and sorrow, of birth and death, as well as the experience of communion with nature. Such a community's way of structuring music may be called naïve, but it does spring from original contact with the fundamental experiences of human existence and is therefore an expression of truth. Its naïveté belongs to that kind of simplicity from which great things can come. Mass society is something completely different from that community bound together for life which produced folk music in the old and original sense. The masses as such do not know experiences firsthand; they only know reproduced and standardized experiences. Mass culture is thus geared to quantity, production, and success. It is a culture of the measurable and marketable. Pop music joins up with this culture. As described by Calvin M. Johansson, it is the reflection of what this society is, the musical embodiment of kitsch.[19] It would be taking things too far to go into Johansson's excellent analysis in detail here, but I would like to recommend it emphatically. Popular in the sense of pop music turns into something for which there is demand. Pop music is manufactured in industrial mass production like technical goods, in a totally inhuman and dictatorial system, as Paul Hindemith says.[20] For melody, harmony, orchestration, and the like, there are specialists at one's disposal who assemble the whole thing according to the laws of the market. Adorno commented: "The fundamental characteristic of popular music is standardization."[21] And

Arthur Korb, whose book title *How to Write Songs That Sell* is already a telltale sign, quite candidly makes the point: popular music "is written and produced primarily to make money."[22] For this reason one has to offer something that does not anger or make profound demands on anyone according to the motto: Give me what I want now—no costs, no work, no effort. Paul Hindemith therefore used the term brainwashing for the constant presence of this kind of noise, which can hardly be called music any more. Johansson adds that it gradually makes us incapable of listening attentively, of hearing; "we become musically comatose."[23]

We still have to show in detail that this fundamental approach is incompatible with the culture of the Gospels, which seek to take us out of the dictatorship of money, of making, of mediocrity, and bring us to the discipline of truth, which is precisely what pop music eschews. Is it a pastoral success when we are capable of following the trend of mass culture and thus share the blame for its making people immature or irresponsible? The medium of communication and the communicated message must stand in a meaningful relationship to each other. As Johansson once again notes, this medium "kills the message."[24] Trivializing faith is not a new inculturation, but the denial of its culture and prostitution with the nonculture.

Openness to Tomorrow
in the Continuity of Faith

Let us admit it: Faith and the culture of faith have a hard time of it in the interstice between aesthetic elitism and industrial mass culture. Their position is difficult simply because art and people themselves have a hard time of it in this situation and can hardly hold their ground. We certainly do not need to inflict upon ourselves the strict discipline the Church practiced in the second and third centuries when, in the face of the gnostic temptation, she reduced church music to the Psalms.

We do not need this if only because, in the meantime, an infinitely larger trove of music that is really appropriate to faith has become available. This trove makes creative attempts to recall and continue [the culture of faith] possible all the time. Undoubtedly we will also have to let considerable tolerance reign on the margins, at the points of transition to the two antitheses of liturgically appropriate music.

But even today it cannot be done without the courage of asceticism, without the courage to contradict. Only from such courage can new creativity arise. We are sure, however, that the creative potency of faith will suffice right up to the end of time: until all the dimensions of the human state have been traversed.

I would like to close my reflections with a quotation from the saintly pope Gregory the Great, which seems to me to formulate the spiritual center of liturgical music in a uniquely beautiful and convincing way.

> If . . . the singing of the psalmody rings out from the innermost reaches of the heart, the omnipotent Lord finds a way through this singing into the heart that he might pour the mysteries of prophecy or the grace of remorse into this attentively listening organ. For it is written: "A song of praise honors me, and this is the way on which I wish to show him the salvation of God" (Ps. 49:23 [cf. NRSV 50:23]). For the Latin *salutare*, salvation, means Jesus in Hebrew. Hence in the song of praise we gain access to where Jesus can reveal himself, for if remorse is poured out through the singing of psalms, then a way to the heart emerges in us at the end of which we reach Jesus."[25]

This is the loftiest service of music through which it does not deny its artistic grandeur but really discovers it to the full. Music uncovers the buried way to the heart, to the core of our being, where it touches the being of the Creator and the Redeemer. Wherever this is achieved, music becomes the road that leads to Jesus, the way on which God shows his salvation.[26]

NOTES

1. A. Deissler, *Die Psalmen* (Düsseldorf, 1964), p. 192.

2. H.-J. Kraus, *Psalmen* (Neukirchen, 1960), 1:348.

3. *La Sainte Bible*, traduite en français sous la direction de l'Ecole biblique de Jérusalem (Paris, 1955), Ps. 47 (46), verse 8: "sonnez pour Dieu de tout votre art!"

4. *Enarrationes in Psalmos*, 32 s 1,8, CCL 38:253–54.

5. See the extremely instructive article *zmr* by Ch. Barth, in *Theological Dictionary of the Old Testament* 4 (1980): 91–98. "The word *zamāru* (= the underlying Akkadian verb) never refers to instrumental 'music' without articulated singing" (p. 92). "In Akkadian, the two meanings 'sing' and 'play' are so firmly linked that it would be more accurate to speak of two aspects of a single meaning: the single action is both 'vocal' and 'instrumental'" (p. 93). "In the long series of words for hymnic praise, *zmr* occupies a middle position, being a term that covers both articulated praise that speaks in comprehensible words and unarticulated praise expressed in shouts and gestures; through it articulated praise takes on a breadth it does not otherwise exhibit, and unarticulated praise acquires a clarity it otherwise lacks" (p. 98). In reference to our verse Barth remarks: "Ps 47:8(7) (*zammerû maśkîl*) remains obscure" (p. 96).

6. M. Hengel, "Das Christuslied im frühesten Gottesdienst," in *Weisheit Gottes, Weisheit der Welt: Festschrift für J. Ratzinger*, ed. W. Baier et al. (St. Ottilien, 1987), 1:357–404 (quotation from p. 387). Ch. Barth (see previous note) has criticized this translation as a one-sided shift in emphasis to the instrumental, and in contrast he noted positively that in Jerome's second version of the Psalter he replaced *psallō* with *cano/canto*. In the process, however, the semantic change in meaning of *psallō* which occurs in the Septuagint is not taken into account.

7. M. Hengel, "Christuslied," p. 388.

8. For interesting information on this point, see H. Gese, "Zur Geschichte der Kultsänger am zweiten Tempel," in *Vom Sinai zum Sion*, 2nd ed. (Munich, 1984), pp. 147–58.

9. See H. Gese, "Psalm 22 und das Neue Testament," in *Vom Sinai zum Sion*, pp. 180–201; idem, "Die Herkunft des Herrenmahls," in *Zur biblischen Theologie* (Munich, 1977), pp. 107–27.

10. See Hengel, "Christuslied" (see n. 6).

11. Exodus 35–40. The parallels between the erection of the sacred tabernacle (Exod. 40:16–33) and the Priestly account of creation (Gen. 1:1–2:4a) are interesting; the seven days of creation correspond to the

sevenfold saying "just as the Lord had commanded Moses"; Gen. 2:1ff is echoed in Exod. 40:33: "So Moses finished the work," which is followed by the theophany (in accord with the sabbath after the six days of creation).

12. H. Gese shows the high theological rank assigned to ritual music in the Old Testament ("Zur Geschichte der Kultsänger" [see n. 8]). There are also helpful comments in P. M. Ernetti, *Principi filosofici e teologici della Musica* (Rome, 1980), vol. 1.

13. See M. Hengel, "Christuslied" (see n. 6), p. 387.

14. Ibid., pp. 382–83.

15. Ibid., pp. 366–70.

16. See the characterization of transcendental Idealism in contrast to the essence of Christian inwardness in H. Kuhn, *Romano Guardini—Philosoph der Sorge* (St. Ottilien, 1987), p. 47, also p. 80.

17. See the next essay in this book, especially the fourth section, "Consequences for Liturgical Music."

18. The essential arguments are carefully presented by M. Basilea Schlink, *Rockmusik—woher, wohin?* (Darmstadt and Eberstadt, 1989); literature is listed there as well. See also U. Bäumer, *Wir wollen nur deine Seele*, 4th ed. (Bielefeld, 1986).

19. C. M. Johansson, *Music and Ministry: A Biblical Counterpoint* (Peabody, Mass. 1984), p. 50. I would emphatically like to endorse this work here which is thorough and balanced in its position, but hitherto unfortunately hardly noticed in Germany.

20. P. Hindemith, *A Composer's World* (Cambridge, 1952), p. 126; quoted in Johansson, *Music*, p. 51.

21. Cited by Johansson, *Music*, p. 52.

22. A. Korb, *How to Write Songs That Sell* (Boston, 1957), p. 8; Johansson, *Music*, p. 53. See also H. Bryce, *How To Make Money Selling the Songs You Write* (New York, 1970).

23. P. Hindemith, *A Composer's World* (see n. 20), pp. 211–12; Johansson, *Music*, p. 49.

24. Johannson, *Music*, p. 55, as a summary of an analysis of the basic spiritual direction of the Christian message on the one hand and of pop music on the other.

25. *Homiliae in Ezechielem I*, hom. 1:15 (*PL* 76:793 A–B). The German translation appears in G. Bürke, *Homilien zu Ezechiel* (Einsiedeln, 1983), p. 45 [translated into English from the German].

26. At about the same time this article appeared the book by Gianfranco Ravasi was published by Piemme—*Il canto della rana: Musica e teologia nella Bibbia* (1990). In the first part of the book there is poetry by D. M. Turoldo under the title "Cantate a Dio con arte" (pp. 7–50); in the second part (pp. 51–163) the well-known exegete G. Ravasi deals

with music and theology in the Bible, with "the musical and the theological," with the silence of music, and finally, under the title "Sound in Pictures," with musical iconography. The author develops his presentation of the music of the Bible from the perspective of our Psalm verse (47:7 [NSRV 47:8]) whose translation "Sing artistically for God" ("Cantate a Dio con arte") he justifies by referring to the commentary on the Psalms by H.-J. Kraus, among others. This brilliantly written work is a treasure trove of insights that I would emphatically like to recommend to the reader.

The Image of the World and of Human Beings in the Liturgy and Its Expression in Church Music

☙

Right from the beginning liturgy and music have been closely related. Wherever people praise God, words alone do not suffice. Conversation with God transcends the boundaries of human speech; everywhere it has, according to its nature, called on music for help, on singing and on the voices of creation in the sound of the instruments. Not only human beings have a role in the praise of God. Worship is singing in unison with that which all things bespeak.

As closely as liturgy and music are related by their very natures, their relationship has been difficult time and again, especially during the transition periods of history and culture. It is therefore no surprise that the question about the right form of music in worship has again become controversial today. In the disputes of the Second Vatican Council and

141

immediately thereafter it seemed to be merely a question of the difference between pastoral practitioners on the one hand and church musicians on the other hand. The musicians did not want to let themselves be subjected to mere pastoral expediency, but tried to show the inner dignity of music as a pastoral and liturgical standard in its own right.[1] The controversy seemed to be taking place essentially on the level of application alone, but the rift goes deeper. The second wave of liturgical reform is pushing the questions forward, as far as the foundations themselves. Here the issue is the essence of liturgical action as such, its anthropological and theological foundations. The controversy about church music has become symptomatic for the deeper question about what liturgical worship is.

SURPASSING THE COUNCIL?
A NEW CONCEPTION OF LITURGY

The new phase of the will to reform liturgically no longer sees its foundation explicitly in the words of the Second Vatican Council, but in its "spirit." As a symptomatic text I shall use the learned and clearly drafted article on song and music in the Church in the *Nuovo Dizionario di Liturgia*. The superior artistic quality of Gregorian chant or of classical polyphony is in no way denied here. It is not even a question of playing off congregational activity against elitist art. Nor is the point the rejection of historical rigidity that only copies the past and thus remains without a present and a future. We are rather concerned with a new, fundamental understanding of liturgy with which one hopes to overtake the Council, whose *Constitution on the Sacred Liturgy* is seen to be of two minds.[2]

Let us briefly try to become acquainted with this conception in its essential features. It states that the starting point for the liturgy is the gathering of two or three who come together in the name of Christ.[3] This reference to the Lord's words of promise in Matt. 18:20 sounds harmless and traditional at first hearing. It receives revolutionary momentum, however, when one isolates this one biblical text and contrasts it with the entire liturgical tradition. For the two or three are then brought into conflict with an institution having institutional roles and with every "codified program." This definition therefore means that the Church does not come before the group, but the group before the Church. It is not the Church as an integral whole that carries the liturgy of the individual group or parish; rather, the group is itself the place of origin for the liturgy. Hence, liturgy does not grow out of a common given either, a "rite" (which now, as a "codified program," has acquired the negative image of lack of freedom); it originates on the spot from the creativity of those gathered. In this specialized language of sociologists, the sacrament of Holy Orders appears as an institutional role that has created a monopoly for itself and dissolves the original unity and community of the group by means of the institution (= the Church).[4] We are told that in this configuration music (just like Latin) then becomes a language of the initiates, "a language of another Church, namely, of the institution and its clergy."[5]

Isolating Matt. 18:20 from the entire biblical and ecclesial tradition of the common prayer of the Church has, as one can see, far-reaching consequences. The Lord's promise to all those praying everywhere is turned into the dogmatization of the autonomous group. The communality of praying is raised to the level of an egalitarianism that sees in the development of the priestly office the emergence of another Church. In such a view, any directive from the whole is a fetter that one must resist for the sake of the originality and freedom of the liturgical celebration. It is not obedience toward the whole but the creativity of the moment that becomes the determining form.

It is evident that with the adoption of sociological language the prior adoption of its evaluations has also occurred. The system of values that sociological language has formed constructs a new view of the past and the present, the one negative, the other positive. Thus, traditional concepts (also conciliar ones!) such as "the wealth of the *musica sacra*," the "organ as queen of the instruments," and the "universality of Gregorian chant" now appear as "mystifications" for the purpose of "preserving a particular form of power."[6] A certain administration of power, we are told, feels threatened by the cultural processes of change and reacts by masking its effort to preserve itself as love for the tradition. Gregorian chant and Palestrina are said to be tutelary gods of a mythicized, ancient repertoire,[7] components of a Catholic counterculture that is based on remythicized and supersacralized archetypes,[8] just as in the historical liturgy of the Church it is generally more a question of representing a cultic bureaucracy than showing concern for the singing activity of the people.[9] Finally, the content of Pius X's *motu proprio* on sacred music is described as a "culturally near-sighted and theologically empty ideology of sacred music."[10] There is of course not only an idolization of sociology at work here but also a complete separation of the New Testament from the history of the Church which is connected to a theory of decline typical of many Enlightenment situations. Purity is found only in the original beginnings with Jesus; all the rest of history appears as a "musical adventure with disoriented and unsuccessful experiences," which we now "must bring to an end" so that we can finally begin again with what is right.[11]

But what do these new and better ideas look like? The leading concepts have already been touched on in passing; we must now pay attention to how they are concretized further. Two basic values are clearly formulated. The "primary value" of a renewed liturgy is, we are told, "the full and authentic action of all persons."[12] Accordingly, church music means first and foremost the following: the "people of God" represents its identity in song. As a result of this statement, the second value judgment operative here is also addressed: music proves to be the power that effects the cohesion of the group; the familiar songs are the identifying mark of a community, so to speak.[13] From this perspective the main categories of the musical structuring of worship ensue: the project, the program, the animation, the direction. We are told that the "how" is more important than the "what."[14] The ability to celebrate is above all "the ability to create"; before all else music must be "created."[15] To be fair I must add that the authors do show a sensitivity for different cultural situations and leave room for the adoption of historical material as well. And, more than anything else, they emphasize the paschal character of the Christian liturgy: the singing of this liturgy not only represents the identity of the people of God but should also give account of our hope and proclaim to all the countenance of the Father of Jesus Christ.[16]

Thus, elements of continuity remain in the deep split. They make discourse possible and instill hope that we can again achieve unity in the basic understanding of the liturgy, although it threatens to disappear through the derivation of the liturgy from the group instead of from the Church—not only theoretically but in concrete liturgical praxis. I would not be speaking of all this in so much detail if I thought that such ideas were attributable to only a few theoreticians. But the belief that the spirit of the Council points in this direction has been able to gain acceptance in many a liturgical office and its agencies, although it is indisputable that these ideas cannot be supported by the text of the Second Vatican Council. In the sense just described, the opinion is all too widely held today that so-called creativity, the active participation of all present, and the relationship to a group in which everyone is acquainted with and speaks to everyone else are the real categories of the conciliar understanding of liturgy. Not only assistant pastors but even some bishops think they are not being faithful to the Council if they pray everything just the way it is found in the Roman Missal; at least *one* "creative" formulation must be inserted, regardless of how trite it may be. And the conventional greeting of the congregation at the beginning along with friendly wishes at the dismissal have already become obligatory elements of the sacred action, which hardly anyone would dare omit.

THE PHILOSOPHICAL BASIS OF THE CONCEPT AND ITS QUESTIONABLE ASPECTS

In considering all this, however, we have not yet touched the core of the change in values. All that has been said up to now results from placing the group before the Church. But why has this been done? The reason is that the Church is categorized under the general term "institution," and, in the type of sociology adopted here, an institution has a negative value in itself. It represents power, and power is regarded as the opposite of freedom. Since faith ("imitation of Christ") is held to be a positive value, it must stand on the side of freedom and thus be anti-institutional by its very nature. For this reason worship should be neither a mainstay nor a component of an institution, but should constitute a counterforce which contributes to dethroning the mighty. From such a starting point the paschal hope, to which the liturgy should be bearing witness, can take on a very earthly form. It turns into the hope that institutions will be overcome, and it itself becomes a means in the struggle against power. Whoever reads the texts of the *Missa Nicaraguensis*, for example, can get an idea of this shift in hope and of the new realism the liturgy acquires as an instrument of militant promise. One also sees the significance that music in fact accrues in the new conception. The stirring power of the revolutionary songs communicates an enthusiasm and a conviction that could not come from a simple spoken liturgy. Here there is no more opposition to liturgical music; it has received a new and irreplaceable role in arousing irrational forces and awakening the communal élan at which the whole thing is aiming. But at the same time it is shaping consciousness, since what is sung gradually communicates itself to the spirit much more effectively than anything that is only spoken or thought. Incidentally, via the liturgy of the group the boundary of the locally assembled parish is again passed over—on purpose: through the liturgical form and its music a new solidarity develops through which a new people is to come into being that calls itself the people of God. But by "God" it only means itself and the historical energies realized in the people.

Let us return once again to the analysis of the values that have become determinative in the new liturgical consciousness. For a start there is the negative quality of the concept "institution" and the fact that the Church is regarded exclusively under this sociological aspect, which is, moreover, not an aspect of empirical sociology, but a point of view that we owe to the so-called masters of suspicion. One sees that they have done their job thoroughly; they have achieved a formation of consciousness that is still effective even where people know nothing of this origin. Suspicion, however, could not have such stirring sway if it were not accompanied by a promise whose fascination is almost irresistible: the idea of freedom as the genuine claim of human dignity. In this respect the question about the right concept of freedom must represent the core of the debate. The controversy over the liturgy has thus moved away from all the superficial questions about its organization and come back to its core, for in the liturgy we are indeed concerned with the presence of redemption, with the access to true freedom. The positive feature of the new debate lies without doubt in its exposure of this as the central issue.

At the same time we can see what Catholicism is suffering from today. If the Church appears only as an institution, as a bearer of power and thus as an opponent of freedom and a hindrance to redemption, then faith is living in a self-contradictory state. For on the one hand it cannot dispense with the Church, but on the other hand it is completely opposed to her. The truly tragic paradox of this trend in liturgical reform lies here. For liturgy without the Church is a self-contradiction. Where all act so that all may themselves become subjects, the One who truly acts in the liturgy also disappears with the collective subject, the Church. Here it has been forgotten that the liturgy should be *opus Dei* in which God himself first acts and we become redeemed people precisely through his action. The group celebrates itself, and exactly for this reason it is celebrating nothing at all since it is no cause for celebration. This is why the general activity turns into boredom. Nothing happens if he is absent whom the world awaits. It is then only logical that one would move on to more concrete goals such as the ones reflected in the *Missa Nicaraguensis*.

We must therefore resolutely ask the proponents of this position: Is the Church really just an institution, a cultic bureaucracy, or an apparatus of power? Is priestly office only the monopolization of sacred privileges? Also, if we do not succeed in overcoming these ideas affectively, succeed in seeing the Church differently again from the heart, then the liturgy is not being renewed; on the contrary, the dead are burying the dead and calling it reform. Neither is there church music any more in this view, since its subject, the Church, has been lost. Indeed, you cannot even rightly speak of liturgy any more, which of course presupposes the Church; what remains are group rituals that make use of musical means of expression with more or less expertise. If liturgy is to survive or even be renewed, it is essential that the Church be rediscovered. I would like to add: If human alienation is to be overcome, if human beings are to find their identity again, it is indispensable that they again find the Church, which is not an institution hostile to humans but that new "we" in which the "I" can first secure its foundation and a place to stay.

In this context it would be salutary to reread carefully the little book with which Romano Guardini, the great pioneer of liturgical renewal, concluded his literary endeavors in the last year of the Council.[17] He wrote this book, as he himself stressed, out of concern and love for the Church whose humanity and whose imperilment he knew very well. But he had learned to discover in the humanity of the Church the scandal of the incarnation of God; he had learned to see in her the presence of the Lord who has made the Church his body. Only if this is the case is Jesus Christ contemporaneous with us. And only if there is this contemporaneity is there real liturgy, which is not just remembrance of the paschal mystery, but its true presence. And once again, only if this is the case is liturgy participation in the trinitarian dialogue of Father, Son, and Holy Spirit; only in this way is it not our "doing," but *opus Dei*—God's action in us and with us. For this reason Guardini emphatically stressed that the important thing in the liturgy is not to do something but to be. The idea that collective activity is the central merit of the liturgy is the most radical antithesis imaginable to Guardini's liturgical conception. In reality, the general activity of everybody is not only not the fundamental value of the liturgy, but as such is not a value at all.[18]

I shall refrain from expanding on these matters any further; we must concentrate on finding the starting point and norm for the right relation of liturgy and music to each other. In this respect the realization that the Church, to be precise, the *communio sanctorum* of all places and all times, is the true subject of the liturgy is really momentous. As Guardini has shown in detail in his earlier work *Liturgische Bildung*,[19] the elusiveness of the liturgy in the face of the willfulness of the group and of individuals (including clerics and specialists), a characteristic that he referred to as the objectivity and positivity of the liturgy, is not the only characteristic that follows from this; above all the three ontological dimensions in which the liturgy lives follow from this: cosmos, history, and mystery. The reference to history involves development, that is, belonging to a living entity which has a beginning that continues to have an effect and stays present but is not completed and lives only by being developed further. Some things die out; some are forgotten only to return later in a new way, but development always means participation in a beginning that is open to what lies ahead. Here we have already touched on a second category that acquires its special meaning through the connection to the cosmos: liturgy understood in this way lives in the basic form of participation. No one is its one and only creator, for each of us it is participation in something greater that transcends us all, yet just in this way each of us is also an agent precisely because each is a recipient. Finally, the relationship to mystery means that the beginning of the liturgical event never lies in us. It is a response to an initiative coming from above, to a call and an act of love which is mystery. Problems are there to be explained; mystery, however, is not open to explanation, but reveals itself only in acceptance, in the yes that we, following the lead of the Bible, may confidently call, even today, obedience.

We have now arrived at a point that is of great importance for the beginnings of what is artistic. The liturgy of the group is not cosmic; it thrives on the autonomy of the group. It does not have a history; precisely the emancipation from history and autonomous creativity are characteristic for group liturgy, even when it works with historical settings in the process. And it does not know mystery because in it everything is and must be explained. For these reasons development and participation are just as foreign to group liturgy as that obedience within which a meaning that is greater than the explicable is revealed. Creativity in which the autonomy of the emancipated tries to prove itself now takes the place of all this. Such creativity, which would like to function as autonomy and emancipation, is for this very reason in strict opposition to all participation. Its characteristics are: arbitrariness as the necessary form of the rejection of each previously given form or norm; unrepeatability because in repetition there would already be dependence; and artificiality, since the result must be a pure creation of humans. In this way, however, it becomes apparent that human creativity that does not want to be receptivity and participation is by its very nature absurd and untrue since humans can only be themselves through receptivity and participation. Such creativity is a flight from the *conditio humana* and therefore untruth. This is the reason why cultural disintegration begins wherever faith in God disappears and a professed *ratio* of being [*Vernunft des Seins*] is automatically called into question.

Let us summarize what we have discovered up to now so that we can then deduce the consequences for the starting point and fundamental form of church music. It has become clear that the primacy of the group stems from an understanding of Church as institution. In turn, this understanding is based on a notion of freedom that does not fit with the idea or the reality of the institutional and is no longer capable of perceiving the dimension of mystery in the reality of the Church. Freedom is understood in terms of the key ideas of autonomy and emancipation. It becomes concrete in the idea of creativity, which in this context is the direct opposite of the objectivity and positivity that belong to the essence of church liturgy. The group is only free if it constantly reinvents itself. At the same time we have seen that a liturgy that deserves the name is radically opposed to this. It is against ahistorical willfulness, which ignores development and thus leads nowhere, and against unrepeatability, which is also exclusiveness and loss of communication despite all group formations. It is not opposed to the technical, but definitely to the artificial, in which humans create a counterworld for themselves and do not see God's creation with their eyes and in their hearts. The oppositions are clear; also clear, at least incipiently, is the inner rationale of this group mentality, which is based on an autonomistically conceived idea of freedom. But now we must ask in a constructive way about the anthropological concept upon which the liturgy as understood by the faith of the Church is based.

THE ANTHROPOLOGICAL MODEL
OF THE CHURCH'S LITURGY

Two pivotal sayings from the Bible provide a key for answering our question. Paul coined the expression *logikē latreia* (Rom. 12:1), which is quite difficult to translate into our modern languages because we do not have a real equivalent for the concept of logos.[20] One could translate it "spiritual worship" and so refer at the same time to the saying of Jesus about worshiping in spirit and truth (John 4:23). One could, however, translate it "divine worship shaped by the word," but would then of course have to add that "word" in the biblical sense (and also the Greek sense) is more than language and speech, namely, creative reality. It is also certainly more than mere thought and mere spirit. It is self-interpreting, self-communicating spirit. At all times the word-orientation, the rationality, the intelligibility, and the sobriety of the Christian liturgy have been derived from this spirit and given to liturgical music as its basic law. It would, however, be a narrow and false interpretation if one understood by this that all liturgical music should be referred to the text in a strict way, and if one would then exaggerate the intelligibility of the text so much that there would be no more room for what is proper to music. For "word" in the sense of the Bible is more than "text," and understanding reaches further than the banal understandability of what is immediately clear to everyone and can be accommodated to the most superficial rationality. But it is correct that music which serves worship "in spirit and truth" cannot be rhythmic ecstasy, sensual intimation or anesthetization, subjective sentimentality, or superficial entertainment; instead it is ordered to a message, to a comprehensive, spiritual, and in the fullest sense rational statement. In other words, it is correct to say that music in a comprehensive sense and deep down inside must correspond to this "word," indeed must serve it.[21]

This leads us automatically to another biblical text, the

truly foundational one concerning the question of cult or worship in which we are told more exactly what the "Word" means and how it relates to us. I am referring to the following sentence in John's Prologue: "And the Word became flesh and lived [pitched his tent] among us, and we have seen his glory" (John 1:14). The "Word" to which Christian worship refers is first of all not a text, but a living reality: a God who is self-communicating meaning and who communicates himself by becoming a human being. This incarnation is the sacred tent, the focal point of all worship which looks at the glory of God and gives him honor. These statements in John's Prologue, however, do not convey everything yet. They have been misunderstood if they are not read together with the farewell discourses in which Jesus tells his followers: I am going, and I will come again to you; by going I am returning; it is good that I go, for only in this way can you receive the Holy Spirit (John 14:2f.; 14:18f.; 16:5ff., etc.). The incarnation is only the first part of the movement. It becomes meaningful and definitive only in the cross and the resurrection. From the cross the Lord draws everything to himself and carries the flesh—that is, humanity and the entire created world—into God's eternity.

Liturgy is ordered to this line of movement, and this line of movement is the fundamental text, so to speak, to which all liturgical music refers, which must measure up to it from the inside. Liturgical music is a result of the claim and the dynamics of the Word's incarnation. For incarnation means that also among us the Word cannot be just speech. To begin with, the sacramental signs themselves are certainly the central way in which the incarnation continues to work. But they would be homeless if they were not immersed in a liturgy that as a whole follows this extension of the Word into the physical and into the sphere of all our senses. The right to have images—indeed their necessity—comes from this in contrast to the Jewish and Islamic types of worship.[22] And from this also comes the necessity to call on those deeper realms of understanding and response that reveal themselves in music. Faith becoming music is a part of the process of the Word becoming flesh. But in a completely unique way this "musification" is at the same time also ordered to that inner shift of the incarnational event that I tried to indicate before: in the cross and the resurrection the incarnation of the Word [*Fleischwerdung des Wortes*] becomes the "verbalization" of the flesh [*Wortwerdung des Fleisches*]. These two pervade each other. The incarnation is not taken back; it only becomes final, so to speak, at the moment the movement is reversed. The flesh becomes "logicized," but precisely this process of the flesh becoming word produces a new unity of all reality, which was obviously so important to God that he let it cost him his Son on the cross. The Word becoming music is on the one hand sensualization, incarnation, the attraction of pre-rational and trans-rational forces, the attraction of the hidden sound of creation, and the uncovering of the song that lies at the base of things. But this musification is also itself now the site of the shift in the movement: it is not only the incarnation of the Word, but at the same time the spiritualization of the flesh. Wood and brass turn into tone; the unconscious and the unsolved become ordered and meaningful sound. An embodiment comes into play that is spiritualization, and a spiritualization occurs that is embodiment. The Christian embodiment is always simultaneously a spiritualization, and the Christian spiritualization is an embodiment into the body of the incarnate Logos.

CONSEQUENCES FOR LITURGICAL MUSIC

Fundamentals

Provided that this interpenetration of both movements occurs in music, it serves to the highest degree and in an indispensable way that inner exodus which liturgy always seeks to be and to become. But this means that the appropriateness of liturgical music is measured by its inner correspondence to this basic anthropological and theological form. At first glance such a statement seems to be very far removed from the concrete reality of music. It becomes concrete immediately, however, if we pay attention to the opposing models of ritual music to which I briefly referred above. For instance, let us think first of all of the Dionysian type of religion and its music, which Plato tackled from his own religious and philosophical point of view.[23] In many forms of religion music is ordered to stupor and to ecstasy. Freeing humans from limitations, which is the goal of that hunger for the infinite proper to humans, is supposed to be achieved through holy madness, through the delirium of the rhythm and the instruments. Such music pulls down the barriers of individuality and personality; in it human beings free themselves from the burden of consciousness. Music turns into ecstasy, liberation from the ego, becoming one with the universe. Today we experience the profane return of this type of music in a large part of the rock and pop music whose festivals are a counter-cult of the same orientation—the pleasure of destruction, the removal of the barriers of everyday life and the illusion of redemption in the liberation from oneself, in the wild ecstasy of noise and the masses. It is a question of redemptive practices whose form of redemption is related to drugs and diametrically opposed to the Christian faith in redemption. Hence it makes sense that in this area satanical cults and satanical types of music are constantly spreading today whose dangerous power intentionally to wreck and eradicate the person has not yet been taken seriously enough.[24] The dispute between Dionysian and Apollonian music with which Plato deals is not ours, since Apollo is not Christ. But the question Plato posed concerns us in a most meaningful way. In a form we could not have imagined a generation ago music has become today the decisive vehicle of a counterreligion and thus the showplace for the discerning of spirits. On the one hand, since rock music seeks redemption by way of liberation from the personality and its responsibility, it fits very precisely into the anarchistic ideas of freedom that are manifesting themselves more openly all over the world. But that is also exactly why such music is diametrically opposed to the Christian notions of redemption and freedom, indeed their true contradiction. Music of this type must be excluded from the Church, not for aesthetic reasons, not out of reactionary stubbornness, not because of historical rigidity, but because of its very nature.

We could concretize our question further if we go on to analyze the anthropological base of different types of music. There is music of provocation, which rouses people for various collective goals. There is sensual music, which drives people into the erotic or is in some other way essentially intent on sensual feelings of pleasure. There is ordinary light music, which does not seek to make a statement, but only wants to break open the burden of silence. There is rationalistic music, in which the tones simply serve rational constructions but no real penetration of the mind and senses ensues. Here one would have to include a number of sterile catechetical songs and modern hymns that have been fabricated in committee. The music that corresponds to the worship of the incarnate One who was raised up on the cross lives from another, greater, and broader synthesis of spirit, intuition, and sensuous sound. We can say that Western music, from Gregorian chant through the music of the cathedrals and great polyphonic music, through Renaissance and baroque music, right up to Bruckner and beyond, derives from the inner richness of this synthesis and has developed its possibilities abundantly. This magnificence exists only here because it was able to grow solely from the anthropological ground that combined the spiritual and the profane in an ultimate human unity. The unity disintegrates to the degree that this anthropology disappears. For me the greatness of this music is the most immediate and most evident verification that history has to offer of the Christian image of human beings and of Christian faith in redemption. Whoever is really touched by it knows somehow deep down inside that the faith is true even if this person still has far to go before comprehending this insight with the mind and will.

This means that the liturgical music of the Church must be subject to that integration of the human state which appears before us in incarnational faith. Such redemption is more arduous than that of rapture, but this struggle is the exertion of truth itself. On the one hand, it must integrate the senses into the spirit; it must correspond to the impulse of the *sursum corda*. On the other hand, however, this effort aims not at pure spiritualization but at an integration of sensuality and spirit so that in one another both become person. It does not debase the spirit when it takes the senses into itself; rather, it supplies the spirit with the whole wealth of creation. Nor does it make the senses less real when they are permeated by the spirit; rather, only in this way do they receive a share in its infinity. Every sensual pleasure is narrowly delimited and ultimately incapable of intensification because the sense act cannot go beyond a certain measure. Whoever expects redemption from it will be disappointed, "frustrated"—as we would say today. But by being integrated into the spirit the senses receive a new depth and reach into the infinity of the spiritual adventure. Only there do they come completely into their own. This, however, presupposes that the spirit as well does not remain closed. The music of faith looks for the integration of the human being in the *sursum corda*; human beings, however, do not find this integration in themselves, but only in the self-transcendence into the incarnate Word. Sacred music that is in the framework of this movement thus becomes a purification of humans, their ascent. But let us not forget that this music is not the work of a moment, but participation in a history. It is realized not by a single individual but only in cooperation. Hence, it is precisely in this music that the entry into the history of faith and the cooperation of all the members of the body of Christ also express themselves. This music leaves behind joy, a higher kind of ecstasy which does not wipe out the person, but unites and thus liberates. It lets us glimpse what freedom is, that freedom which does not destroy, but gathers and purifies.

Comments on the Present Situation

The question for the musician is now, of course: How does one do this? In principle, great works of church music can be bestowed only because the self-transcendence involved cannot be achieved by humans alone, whereas a delirium of the senses is producible according to the known mechanisms of intoxication. Producing stops where the truly great begins. We must first of all see and accept this boundary. In this respect, at the beginning of great sacred music there is of necessity awe, receptivity, and a humility that is prepared to serve by participating in the greatness which has already gone forth. Only one who lives through and through from the inner structure of this image of the human being can create the music that belongs to this image.

The Church has put up two further road signs. Liturgical music must in its inner character meet the requirements of the great liturgical texts—the *Kyrie, Gloria, Credo, Sanctus, Agnus Dei*. As I have already said, this does not mean that it can only be text music, but it does find a guide for its own message in the inner orientation of these texts. The second road sign is the reference to Gregorian chant and to Palestrina. Once again, this does not mean that all church music has to be imitation of this music. On this point there was indeed a certain narrowness in the renewal of church music during the last century and probably also in the papal documents based on this renewal. Correctly understood, we are simply saying that models were given here that provide orientation. What can arise through the creative application of such an orientation cannot, however, be decided in advance.

The question remains: Humanly speaking can we hope that new creative possibilities are still open here? And how is this to happen? The first question is actually easy to answer. If this image of the human being is inexhaustible in contrast to every other image, then it also opens ever new possibilities to artistic expression. And the more the possibilities, the more vitally will it define the spirit of an age. But herein lies the difficulty for the second question. In our age faith has largely disappeared as a publicly formative force. How is it to become creative? Has it not been driven back everywhere into being a mere subculture? In response we could say that certainly in Africa, Asia, and Latin America we can hope for a new flowering of the faith from which new forms of culture could sprout. But even in the Western world the word "subculture" should not frighten us. In the crisis of culture we are experiencing, it is only from islands of spiritual concentration that a new cultural purification and unification can break out at all. Wherever faith reawakens in lively communities we also see how Christian culture develops anew, how the communal experience provides inspiration and opens new paths that we could not see before. Furthermore, J. F. Doppelbauer has correctly pointed out that often and not incidentally liturgical music actually has a mature quality about it and presupposes that a process of growth has already taken place.[25] Here it is important that there are the antechambers of popular piety and its music as well as spiritual music in the broader sense, which should always be involved in a fertile exchange with liturgical music. Popular spiritual music will be enriched and purified by liturgical music on the one hand but will also prepare new styles of liturgical music. From the freer popular forms there can then mature what can join the common ground of the universal worship of the Church. This is also the area in which the group can test its creativity in the hope that what grows from this may one day belong to the whole.[26]

A FINAL WORD:
LITURGY, MUSIC, AND COSMOS

At the end of my reflections I would like to note a beautiful saying of Mahatma Gandhi that I recently found in a calendar. Gandhi refers to the three habitats of the cosmos and how each of these provides its own mode of being. The fish live in the sea, and they are silent. The animals of the earth scream and shout; but the birds, whose habitat is the heavens, sing. Silence is proper to the sea, shouting to the earth, and singing to the heavens. Human beings have a share in all three of them. They carry the depths of the sea, the burden of the earth, and the heights of the heavens in themselves, and for this reason all three properties also belong to them: silence, shouting, and singing. Today—I would like to add—we see that only the shouting is left for those humans without transcendence since they only want to be earth and also try to make the heavens and the depths of the sea into their earth. The right liturgy, the liturgy of the communion of saints, restores totality to these people. It teaches them silence and singing again by opening to them the depths of the sea and teaching them to fly, the angels' mode of being. It brings the song buried in them to sound once more by lifting up their hearts. Indeed, we can now even turn this around and say: One recognizes right liturgy by the fact that it liberates us from ordinary, everyday activity and returns to us once more the depths and the heights, silence and song. One recognizes right liturgy in that it has a cosmic, not just a group, character. It sings with the angels. It is silent with the expectant depths of the universe. And that is how it redeems the earth.

NOTES

1. See J. Ratzinger, *The Feast of Faith*, trans. Graham Harrison (San Francisco: Ignatius Press, 1986), pp. 97–126.

2. F. Rainoldi and E. Costa, Jr., "Canto e musica," *Nuovo Dizionario di Liturgia*, ed. D. Sartore und A. M. Triacca (Rome, 1984), pp. 198–219; especially p. 211a: ". . . i documenti del Vaticano II rivelano l'esistenza di due anime . . ."; and p. 212a: "Queste serie di spunti, dedotti dallo spirito più che dalla lettera del Vaticano II. . . ."

3. Ibid., p. 199a.

4. Ibid., p. 206b.

5. Ibid., p. 204a: "La celebrazione si configura come splendido 'opus' cui assistere e ai suoi protagonisti si riconoscono poteri misteriosi: cosi lo stacco culturale comincia a diventare stacco 'sacrale'. . . . La musica si avvia a diventare, come il latino, una 'lingua' colta: la lingua di un'altra chiesa, che è l'istituzione ed il suo clero."

6. Ibid., p. 200a: "Si pensi . . . alla ripetività di schemi mentali e giudizi preconfezionati; all'affabulazione-occultamento di dati per sostenere una determinata forma di potere e di visione ideologica. Si pensi ad espressioni mistificatorie correnti come: 'il grando patrimonio della musica sacra'; 'il pensiero della chiesa sul canto'; 'l'organo re degli strumenti'; 'l'universalità del canto gregoriano' ecc."; see also pp. 210b, 206b.

7. Ibid., p. 210b.

8. Ibid., p. 208a.

9. Ibid., p. 206a.

10. Ibid., p. 211a.

11. Ibid., p. 212a.

12. Ibid., p. 211b.

13. Ibid., p. 217b.

14. Ibid., p. 217b.

15. Ibid., p. 218b: ". . . i membri dell'assemblea credente, e soprattutto gli animatori del rito . . . sapranno acquistare . . . quella capacità fondamentale, che è il 'saper celebrare,' ossia un saper fare. . . ."

16. Ibid., p. 212a.

17. R. Guardini, *Die Kirche des Herrn: Meditationen* (Würzburg, 1965) [Eng.: *The Church of the Lord* . . . , trans. Stella Lange (Chicago: H. Regnery, 1967)]. Guardini comments here on the "opening," which is just in progress; he welcomes it, but at the same time he also shows what its inner criterion is: "May the events of the present not lead to a trivialization or a softening of the Church, but may it ever stand clearly in our consciousness that the Church is a 'mystery' and a 'rock'" (p. 18). He comments briefly on both concepts, tracing the concept "rock" back to that of truth; from the claim of truth follows that the Church must stand "unshakable in the distinction between true and false in spite of all her ties to the times . . . since only the truth and the demand for the truth mean genuine respect, whereas compliance and

accepting-anything-else-as-well is weakness, which does not dare to challenge humans with the majesty of the self-revealing God; basically it is contempt of humans" [translated into English from the German]. In this context one should also reread the *Méditation sur l'Eglise* by H. de Lubac [Eng.: *The Splendor of the Church*, trans. Michael Mason from the 2nd ed. (San Francisco: Ignatius Press, 1986)], which has appeared in a new French edition (Paris, 1985).

18. I have tried to give more details about Guardini's understanding of the liturgy in the chapter "Von der Liturgie zur Christologie," of my book *Wege zur Wahrheit: Die bleibende Bedeutung von R. Guardini* (Düsseldorf, 1985), pp. 121–44.

19. R. Guardini, *Liturgische Bildung: Versuche* (Rotenfels, 1923); revised new edition under the title *Liturgie und liturgische Bildung* (Würzburg, 1966).

20. [The heading for Part II, "Worship in Accord with the Logos," is based on this verse. There Ratzinger renders *logikē latreia* as *logos-gemäßer Gottesdienst.—Trans.*]

21. For a proper understanding of the Pauline *logikē latreia*, see especially H. Schlier, *Der Römerbrief* (Freiburg, 1977), pp. 350–58, particularly pp. 356–58.

22. See the thorough work of Chr. Schönborn, *Die Christus-Ikon* (Schaffhausen, 1984) [Eng.: *God's Human Face: The Christ Icon* (San Francisco: Ignatius Press, 1994)].

23. See J. Ratzinger, *The Feast of Faith* (see n. 1); A. Rivaud, "Platon et la musique," *Rev. d'histoire de la philosophie* (1929): 1–30.

24. These connections, which have been much too little noticed, have been emphasized in the writings of Bob Larson, a former disc jockey and leader of a rock band: *Rock and Roll: The Devil's Diversion* (1967); *Rock and the Church* (1971); *Hippies, Hindus and Rock and Roll* (1972). Concerning music from the realm of jazz and pop, which is perhaps less harmful but opposed to the liturgy in essentially the same way, see H. J. Burbach, "Sacro-Pop," *Internationale katholische Zeitschrift Communio* 3 (1974): 91–94. "'Sacro-pop,' posing here as avantgarde, is the product of a 'dirigiste mass culture' which reproduces the cheap taste of the lowbrow consumer public" (p. 94). See also idem, "Aufgaben und Versuche," in *Geschichte der katholische Kirchenmusik*, ed. R. G. Fellerer (Kassel, 1976), 2:395–405. In sum, Burbach concludes: "It is a question of music which tends toward a constantly advancing liquidation of the individual, especially in its 'rhythm,' and does this in a world that is moving toward total management by virtue of the concentration of ever larger power complexes. Music becomes an ideology. It steers, regulates, filters, and combines a stream of feelings

that at first lacks direction. The music restricts this stream to sterotyped patterns of experience" (p. 404).

25. J. F. Doppelbauer, "Die geistliche Musik und die Kirche," *Internationale katholische Zeitschrift Communio* 13 (1984): 457–66.

26. Important for the theological and musical foundations of church music, which have only been mentioned briefly here, is J. Overath, "Kirchenmusik im Dienst des Kultes," *Internationale katholische Zeitschrift Communio* 13 (1984): 355–68; a very extensive panorama of ideas can be found in P.-W. Scheele, "Die liturgische und apostolische Sendung der Musica sacra," *Musica sacra: Zeitschrift des allgemeinen Cäcilienverbandes für die Länder deutscher Sprache* 105 (1985): 187–207.

8

"In the Presence of the Angels I Will Sing Your Praise": The Regensburg Tradition and the Reform of the Liturgy

ꙮ

EARTHLY AND HEAVENLY LITURGY: THE VIEW OF THE FATHERS

After an unforgettable helicopter flight over the mountains of South Tyrol in the fall of 1992,[1] I was able to visit the monastery of Marienberg in the Vinschgau, which was founded there in magnificent scenery in praise of God, thus embracing in its own way the invitation of the three young men: "You mountains and hills, praise the Lord" (Dan. 3:75 [NRSV Prayer of Azariah v. 53]). The real treasure of the monastery is the crypt, consecrated on July 13, 1160, with its marvelous frescoes, which have since been almost completely laid open to view.[2] As with all medieval art, the pictures were not just of aesthetic import. They can be seen as liturgy, as part of the great liturgy of creation and of the redeemed

164

world; the monastery was founded to harmonize with this liturgy. The iconography therefore corresponds to the common fundamental understanding of liturgy still alive in the entire Church—East and West. It exhibits a strong Byzantine influence, but at its core it is quite simply biblical and, in another respect, considerably determined by the monastic tradition, specifically by the Rule of St. Benedict.

For this reason the real focal point is the *Majestas Domini*, the risen Lord lifted up on high, who is seen at the same time and above all as the one returning, the one already coming in the Eucharist. In the celebration of the liturgy the Church moves toward the Lord; liturgy is virtually this act of approaching his coming. In the liturgy the Lord is already anticipating his promised coming. Liturgy is anticipated Parousia, the "already" entering our "not yet," as John described it in the account of the wedding at Cana. The hour of the Lord has not yet come; all that must happen is not yet fulfilled; but at Mary's—the Church's—request Jesus does give the new wine now and already bestows in advance the gift of his hour.

The risen Lord is not alone. In the images of the heavenly liturgy given in the Apocalypse of John he is surrounded by the four creatures and above all by a host of singing angels. Their singing is an expression of a joy that cannot be taken away, of existence releasing itself into the jubilation of fulfilled freedom. From the beginning, monasticism was understood as living in the manner of the angels, and the manner of the angels is worshiping. To enter the angels' way of life means forming life into worship as far as human frailty allows.[3] Thus, the liturgy is the center of monasticism, but monasticism only makes visible for all what the point of Christian existence, indeed of human existence really is. When the monks of Marienberg saw these frescoes, they certainly thought of the nineteenth chapter of the Rule of St. Benedict— the discipline of singing the Psalms—where, among other things, the father of the monks reminds them of Ps. 137:1

[NRSV Ps. 138:1]: "In the presence of the angels I will sing to you." Benedict goes on to say: "Let us reflect upon how we should be in the presence of God and the angels, and when we sing let us stand in such a way that our hearts are in tune with our voices—*mens nostra concordet voci nostrae*." Hence, it is not the case that you think something up and then sing it; instead, the song comes to you from the angels, and you have to lift up your heart so that it may be in tune with the music coming to it. But above all else this is important: the liturgy is not a thing the monks create. It is already there before them. It is entering into the liturgy of the heavens that has always been taking place. Earthly liturgy is liturgy because and only because it joins what is already in process, the greater reality. Thus, the meaning of the frescoes becomes completely clear. Through them the true reality, the heavenly liturgy, looks into this space; they are the window, as it were, through which the monks look out and look into the great heavenly choir. To sing with this choir is the essence of their calling. "In the presence of the angels I will sing your praise"—through the frescoes this ideal stands forever present before their eyes.

HIGHLIGHTING THE POSTCONCILIAR DISPUTE ON THE LITURGY

Let us climb down from Marienberg and the views and insights it affords into the plain of the ordinary life of liturgy today. The panorama here is far more confusing. Harald Schützeichel has described the situation today as an "already and not yet." This no longer describes the eschatological anticipation of the coming of Christ in a world still marked by death and its tribulations; rather, the new that is "already" present is now the reform of the liturgy, but the old—the Tridentine order—has "not yet" been overcome.[4] Thus, the question Where shall I turn? is no longer, as it once was, a search for the countenance of the living God, but a description of the helpless plight of church music that has resulted from the halfhearted realization of liturgical reform. A momentous change of perspectives has obviously occurred here. A chasm separates the history of the Church into two irreconcilable worlds: the preconciliar and the postconciliar. Indeed, in many circles there is no worse verdict than being able to say that a Church decision, a text, a particular structuring of the liturgy, or a person is "preconciliar." Accordingly, Catholicism must have been imprisoned in a truly dreadful situation until 1965.

Let us apply this to the practical case at hand. If this is the case, then a cathedral choirmaster who carried out his duties in the Regensburg cathedral from 1964 to 1994 found himself in a rather hopeless situation. When he began, the *Constitution on the Sacred Liturgy* of the Second Vatican Council had not yet been implemented. At the time he assumed office, he was still quite clearly subject to the standard of the Regensburg tradition that had been established with understandable pride, or, to put it more precisely, of the *motu proprio* "Tra le sollecitudini" on the question of sacred music, which was promulgated by Pius X on November 22, 1903.[5] Nowhere had this *motu proprio* been so joyfully received, so unconditionally accepted as norm as in the Regensburg cathedral, which became with this stance exemplary for many cathedrals and parishes in Germany and beyond. In this reform of church music, Pius X had made use of his own knowledge and experience of the liturgy. As bishop of Mantua and patriarch of Venice he had fought against the operatic church music that was dominant in Italy at that time. Insisting on chant as the truly liturgical music was for him part of a larger reform program that was concerned with restoring to worship its purity and dignity and shaping it according to its own inner claim.[6] In his endeavors he had come to know the Regensburg tradition which represented one of the godparents for the *motu proprio*, although this did not lead to its being canonized as such and as a whole. In Germany today Pius X is seen only as the antimodernist pope. In his critical biography Gianpaolo Romanato has clearly shown how much this pope of pastoral care was a pope of reform.[7]

For someone who takes all this into consideration and looks at it a little more closely, the chasm between preconciliar and postconciliar already becomes narrower. The historian will add a further insight. The *Constitution on the Sacred Liturgy* did indeed lay the foundations for reform; the reform itself was then shaped by a postconciliar commission and cannot in its concrete details simply be credited to the Council. The Council was an ambitious beginning whose large framework permitted a variety of actualizations. If one considers all this properly, one would describe the poles of tension that developed during these decades not as preconciliar tradition and conciliar reform but more accurately as the reform of Pius X and the reform initiated by the Council, that is, stages of reform, not a chasm between two worlds. If we expand this view even further, then we can say that the history of liturgy always stands in the tension between continuity and renewal. It is always growing into new todays, and it must constantly prune the today that has become yesterday, so that what is essential may appear vigorous and new. Liturgy needs growth as well as cleansing, and the preservation of its identity is crucial. Without this, liturgy would lose its very raison d'être, the ground of its being. But if this is the case, then the alternative between traditional forces and reformers is oversimplified. Those who think that we can choose only between the old and the new are barking up the wrong tree. The question is rather: What is liturgy by its very nature? Which standard does it establish on its own? Only when this is clarified can we go on to ask: What must remain? What can and what should perhaps be different?

On the Essence of Liturgy and
the Criteria of Reform

In the frescoes of Marienberg we found an initial, preconceptual answer to the question of the essence of liturgy which must now be developed further. In this endeavor we run into one of the alternatives which stems from the dualistic historical view of a pre- and postconciliar world. According to this alternative, the priest alone was the celebrant of the liturgy before the Council, but since the Council it is the assembled congregation. Therefore—so the conclusion—the congregation as the true subject determines what happens in the liturgy.[8] The priest, of course, never had the right to determine by himself what was to be done in the liturgy. Liturgy was completely nonarbitrary for him. It preceded him as "rite," that is, as an objective form of the corporate prayer of the Church.

The polemical alternative "priest or congregation as celebrant of the liturgy" is absurd; it obstructs an understanding of the liturgy instead of promoting it, and it creates that false rift between preconciliar and postconciliar which rends the overarching coherence of the living history of the faith. It is based on a superficial kind of thinking in which the real issue no longer appears at all. In contrast, if we open the *Catechism of the Catholic Church*, we find the sum of the best insights of the Liturgical Movement put in a masterly concise and clear way, and as a result we find the permanent and the valid things that this great tradition contains. First we are reminded that liturgy means "service in the name of/on behalf of the people."[9] When Christian theology adopted this word from the Greek Old Testament, a word that had been coined in the pagan world, it naturally thought of the People of God, who Christians had become by Christ's having torn open the wall between Jews and pagans to unite them all in the peace of the one God. "Service on behalf of the people"—the theologians remembered that this people did not exist on its own at all, for instance, through a community of common descent, but that it only came into existence through the paschal service of Jesus Christ and is thus based on the service of another, the Son. The People of God is not simply there, as the Germans, French, Italians, or other peoples are; it comes into being again and again only through the service of the Son and by his lifting us into the community of God which we cannot enter on our own. Accordingly, the *Catechism* continues: "In Christian tradition it (the word 'liturgy') means the participation of the People of God in 'the work of God.'" The *Catechism* quotes the *Constitution on the Sacred Liturgy,* which states that every liturgical celebration is an action of Christ the priest and his Body which is the Church.[10]

Now the situation really looks quite different. The sociological reduction that can compare human protagonists only with each other has been done away with. Liturgy presupposes—as we have seen—that the heavens have been opened; only if this is the case is there liturgy at all. If the heavens are not open, then whatever liturgy was is reduced to role playing and, in the end, to a trivial pursuit of congregational self-fulfillment in which nothing really happens. The decisive factor, therefore, is the primacy of Christology. Liturgy is God's work or it does not exist at all. With this "first" of God and of his action, which looks for us in earthly signs, the universality of all liturgy and its universal public nature are given; we cannot comprehend them from the category of congregation, but only from the categories of people of God and body of Christ. Only in this large framework is the reciprocal relation of priest and congregation correctly understood. In the liturgy the priest says and does what he cannot do and say on his own; he acts—as the tradition expresses it—*in persona Christi,* that is, from the sacrament which vouches for the presence of the other, of Christ. He does not represent himself, nor is he a delegate of the congregation that has assigned him a role, as it were. Rather, his standing in the sacrament of imitation, of following, expresses precisely that "first" of Christ which is the fundamental condition of all liturgy. Since the priest represents this "first" of Christ, he refers each gathering to a point beyond itself into the whole, for Christ is only one and, by opening up the heavens, he is also the one who does away with all earthly limitations.

The *Catechism* structures its theology of the liturgy in a trinitarian way. I think it is very important that the congregation, the assembly, appears in the chapter on the Holy Spirit; there it states:

> In the *liturgy of the New Covenant* every liturgical action, especially the celebration of the Eucharist and the sacraments, is an encounter between Christ and the Church. The liturgical community [*die Gemeinde*, CCC "assembly"] derives its unity from the "communion [*die Gemeinschaft*] of the Holy Spirit" who gathers the children of God into the one Body of Christ. This assembly transcends racial, cultural, social—indeed, all human affinities. The assembly should *prepare* itself to encounter its Lord and to become "a people well disposed."[11]

It should be recalled that the German word *Gemeinde*—which dates from the tradition of the Reformation [and is related to the Latin word *communio*]—cannot be translated into most languages. Its equivalent in the romance languages is *assemblée* ("assembly or gathering"), which already emphasizes a slightly different aspect. Two important features are indisputably addressed by both expressions (community, assembly): (1) that the participants of the liturgical celebration are not unrelated individuals but are joined together through the liturgical event into a concrete representation of the People of God; (2) that as the People of God assembled here they are by virtue of the Lord active co-celebrants of the liturgical event. But we must resolutely defend ourselves against the hypostatization of the community, which is common today. As the *Catechism* rightly states, the assembled derive their unity from the communion of the Holy Spirit; they are not such on their own, as a sociologically self-contained quantity. But when they stand in a unity derived from the Spirit, it is always an open unity whose transcendence of racial, cultural, and social barriers is expressed in concrete openness to those who do not belong to the core group. Today's talk about community presupposes to a large extent a homogeneous group that can plan and execute common activities. This "community" could probably be expected to accept only a priest who knows it and whom it knows. All this has nothing to do with theology. When, for example, people who definitely do not form a uniform group in the sociological sense and who can, for instance, only with difficulty join together in common song, when these people are gathered for solemn worship in a large cathedral, are they a community or not? Yes, they are because the common turning to the Lord in faith and the Lord's coming toward them unite these people inwardly much more deeply than a mere social sense of solidarity could effect. In sum we can say that neither the priest alone nor the community alone is the celebrant of the liturgy, but the whole Christ is the celebrant, head and members. The priest, the assembly, and the single individuals are all celebrant insofar as they are united with Christ and insofar as they represent him in the communion of head and body. In every liturgical celebration the whole Church—heaven and earth, God and humans—is involved, not just theoretically but in a wholly real manner. The more the celebration is nourished from this knowledge and from this experience, the more concretely will the liturgy become meaningful.

With these reflections we have seemingly strayed quite far from the subject of the Regensburg tradition and postconciliar reform, but only seemingly. This large framework had to come into view since each reform is judged by it, and only from its perspective can we adequately describe the inner place and the right style of church music. Now we can say in brief what the essential tendency of the reform chosen by the Council was. In the face of modern individualism and the moralism connected with it, the dimension of mystery was supposed to reappear, that is, the cosmic character of liturgy that embraces heaven and earth. In its participation in the paschal mystery of Christ, liturgy transcends the boundaries of places and times in order to gather all into the hour of Christ that is anticipated in the liturgy and hence opens history to its goal.[12]

Two further points are added in the liturgical constitution of Vatican II. In the Christian faith the concept of mystery is inseparable from that of Logos. In contrast to many pagan mystery cults, the Christian mysteries are Logos-mysteries. They go beyond human reason, but instead of leading to the formlessness of intoxication or to the dissolution of reason into an irrationally understood cosmos, they lead to Logos, that is, to the creative reason on which the meaning of all things is based. The ultimate sobriety, rationality, and verbal character of the liturgy come from this. A second element is connected to it: the Logos has become flesh in history; for Christians, therefore, orientation toward the Logos is also always orientation toward the historical origin of faith, toward the biblical word and its normative development in the Church of the Fathers. From looking at the mystery of a cosmic liturgy which is Logos-liturgy there arose the necessity to represent the character of worship as communion, its character as action, and its determination as word in a visible and concrete way; all the individual instructions for the revision of books and rites are to be understood on this basis. If this is kept in mind, then it turns out that the Regensburg tradition as well as the *motu proprio* of Pius X point in the same direction with the same intent in spite of external differences. Dismantling the orchestral apparatus, which had evolved into operatic dimensions particularly in Italy, was supposed to place music completely at the service of the liturgical word and at the service of worship again. Church music was no longer supposed to be a performance on the occasion of worship, but was to be liturgy itself, that is, a harmonizing with the choir of the angels and saints. Thus, it was supposed to become transparent that liturgical music leads the faithful straight to the glorification of God, into the sober intoxication of the faith. The emphasis on Gregorian chant and classical polyphonic music was therefore ordered to both the character of the liturgy as mystery and its character as Logos, as well as to its bond to the historical word. It was supposed to bring out the normativeness of the Fathers, so to speak, which had perhaps at times been interpreted in a too exclusive and too historicized way. Normativity, when properly understood, does not mean the exclusion of the new, but guidance which points one toward what lies on the horizon. Striding forth into new country is made possible here precisely by the fact that the right path has been found. Only when one understands that the reforms of Pius and the Council have this intention and this direction essentially in common can correctly evaluate the differences in their practical instructions. Conversely, we can then say that viewing the liturgy while blind to its character as mystery and its cosmic dimension necessarily causes not reform but deformation of the liturgy to occur.

FOUNDATION AND ROLE
OF MUSIC IN WORSHIP

The question concerning the essence of liturgy and the criteria of reform has automatically brought us back to the question concerning the place of music in liturgy. As a matter of fact, one cannot speak of liturgy without also talking about the music of worship. Where liturgy deteriorates, the *musica sacra* also deteriorates, and where liturgy is correctly understood and lived, there good church music also grows. We have already seen that the concept of "community," or "assembly," first appears in the *Catechism* where the Holy Spirit is spoken of as the one who gives the liturgy its shape;

we said that thereby the inner place of the assembly is exactly delineated. It is no coincidence either that the phrase "to sing" first appears where the cosmic nature of the liturgy is under consideration—to be precise, in a quotation from the *Constitution on the Sacred Liturgy* of the Second Vatican Council: "In the earthly liturgy we share in a foretaste of that heavenly liturgy which is celebrated in the Holy City of Jerusalem toward which we journey as pilgrims. . . . With all the warriors of the heavenly army we sing a hymn of glory to the Lord."[13] Philipp Harnoncourt has expressed the same point very beautifully by adapting Wittgenstein's saying "What one cannot talk about one must remain silent about" as follows: "What one cannot talk about one can, indeed must, sing and make music about if one cannot be silenced."[14] Somewhat later he adds: "Jews and Christians agree with one another that their singing and music-making point to heaven, or rather that these come from heaven or are learned from heaven."[15] The fundamental principles of liturgical music are given already in these sentences. Faith comes from listening to God's word. But wherever God's word is translated into human words there remains a surplus of the unspoken and unspeakable which calls us to silence—into a silence that in the end lets the unspeakable become song and also calls on the voices of the cosmos for help so that the unspoken may become audible. This means that church music, coming from the Word and the silence perceived in it, always presupposes a new listening to the whole richness of the Logos.

Whereas Schützeichel maintains that in principle every kind of music could be used in religious service,[16] Harnoncourt refers to more profound and fundamental connections between particular actions in life and the musical expressions appropriate to them; he goes on to say: "For the encounter with the mystery of faith I am convinced that there is . . . in a certain way appropriate, or also inappropriate music."[17] As a matter of fact, music that is supposed to serve the Christian liturgy must correspond to the Logos, concretely. It must stand in a meaningful relation to the words in which the Logos has expressed himself. It cannot free itself, not even as instrumental music, from the inner orientation of these words, which open up endless space, but also draw distinctions. By its nature such music must be different from music that is supposed to lead to rhythmic ecstasy, stupifying anesthetization, sensual excitement, or dissolution of the ego in Nirvana, to name just a few possibilities. On this point there is a lovely saying in St. Cyprian's interpretation of the Our Father:

> Discipline, which includes tranquility and awe, belongs to the words and posture of praying. We should be mindful that we are standing before the eyes of God. One must please the divine eyes through the posture of the body and the implementation of its voice. Shamelessness expresses itself in vulgar shouting; it is proper for the reverent one to pray in timid words. . . . When we come together as one with our brothers and celebrate the divine sacrifice with the priest, we must not stir the air with formless sounds nor fling our petitions to God with extensive palaver which should instead be humbly commended to him because God . . . does not need to be reminded through our shouting.[18]

Naturally this internal norm of music in accord with the Logos must be grounded. It must show people here and now, at this time and in this place, as prayers into Christ's communion. It has to be accessible to them but at the same time lead them further, and lead them further exactly in that direction which the liturgy itself indicates in a matchlessly brief formula at the beginning of the Preface: *sursum corda*—the heart, that is, the inner person, the entirety of the self, lifted up into the height of God, to that height which is God and which in Christ touches the earth, draws it to itself and pulls it up to itself.

CHOIR AND CONGREGATION:
THE QUESTION OF LANGUAGE

Before I try to apply these principles to a few specific problems of church music in the Regensburg cathedral, there is still something to say about the subjects of liturgical music and the language of hymns. Where an exaggerated and, especially in our mobile society (as we were able to establish), completely unrealistic concept of congregation prevails, only the priest and congregation can be acknowledged as the legitimate singers of liturgical hymns. The primitive actionism and prosaic pedagogical rationalism of such a position have generally been seen through today and are therefore only rarely maintained. That a schola and choir can also contribute to the whole is seldom challenged, not even where one falsely interprets the conciliar phrase "active participation" in the sense of an external actionism. Admittedly, vetoes against the use of a choir remain, which we will consider in a moment. They are based on an inadequate interpretation of liturgical togetherness. In this togetherness the present congregation can never simply be the subject; rather, it must be understood as an assembly that is open upwards and open synchronically and diachronically into the wide expanse of God's history. Once again Harnoncourt has brought an important point into play when he speaks of elevated forms that cannot be missing in the liturgy as God's celebration, but whose high demands cannot be satisfied by the congregation as a whole. He goes on to say: "The choir, therefore, is not standing before a community which is listening like an audience that lets itself be sung to, but is itself part of the community and sings for it in the sense of legitimately representing it or standing in for it."[19] The concept of representation, of standing in for another, which affects all levels of religious reality and is thus also important in the liturgical assembly in particular, is one of the fundamental categories of Christian faith as a whole.[20] The insight that this is a matter of representation does indeed eliminate the rivalry of the other side. The choir acts for the others and includes them in its own action in this "for." Through its singing everyone can be led into the great liturgy of the communion of saints and thus into that kind of praying which pulls our hearts upwards and lets us join, above and beyond all earthly realizations, the heavenly Jerusalem.

But are we really allowed to sing in Latin if the people do not understand it? After the Council a fanaticism about vernacular appeared in a number of places, which is actually abstruse in a multicultural society, just as the hypostatization of the community in a mobile society has no logic to it. Let us first disregard the fact that a text is not yet understandable to everyone just because it has been translated into each person's mother tongue, even though we have touched on a question of no little importance here. Once again Philipp Harnoncourt has described in an excellent fashion an aspect that is essential for Christian liturgy in general:

> This celebration is not interrupted as soon as something is sung or played by instruments . . . ; on the contrary, it displays its "celebratory" character precisely in this. This requirement, however, demands neither uniformity in liturgical language nor uniformity in the style of the musical parts. The traditional, so-called "Latin Mass" always had Aramaic (*Amen, Alleluia, Hosanna, Maran atha*) and Greek (*Kyrie eleison, Trisagion*) parts, and the sermon was usually given in the vernacular. Real life is not acquainted with stylistic unity and perfection; on the contrary, where something is really alive formal and stylistic variety will occur . . . , and the unity is an organic one.[21]

In the thirty years of theological and liturgical upheaval during which he was given the task of discharging his duties, the departing cathedral choirmaster has known, from the perspective of these insights, how to manage continuity in development and development in continuity, quite frequently in the headwind of tremendously pretentious trends. In this he was supported by the confidence of Bishop Graber as well as of his successor, Bishop Manfred Müller and the auxiliary bishops Flügel, Guggenberger, and Schraml. Thanks to this deep rapport with the responsible bishops and their staff he could contribute considerably and in a steadfast, yet open way so that the liturgy in the Regensburg cathedral kept its dignity and excellence and remained transparent to the cosmic liturgy of the Logos in the unity of the whole Church without taking on a museumlike character or turning into a nostalgic fossil in the shadows. In conclusion I would like to examine briefly, and also contrary to prevailing opinions, two characteristic examples of this struggle for continuity in development: the issue of the *Sanctus* and *Benedictus* and the question about the appropriate place for the *Agnus Dei*.

SPECIFIC QUESTIONS:
SANCTUS—BENEDICTUS—AGNUS DEI

My former Münster colleague and friend E. J. Lengeling has said, if one understands the *Sanctus* as an authentic part for the congregation celebrating Mass, "then this not only leads to compelling conclusions for new musical settings, but also results in vetoes for most of the Gregorian and for all the polyphonic versions since they exclude the people from singing and do not take the character of acclamation into account."[22] With all due respect for the eminent liturgist, his opinion shows that even experts can be wide of the mark. First of all, mistrust is always in order when a large part of the living history has to be thrown onto the garbage dump of discarded misunderstandings. This is all the more true for the Christian liturgy, which lives from the continuity and inner unity of the history of religious prayer. In fact, the assertion that the acclamatory character can be attended to only by the congregation is completely unfounded. In the entire liturgical tradition of the East and the West, the Preface always closes with the reference to the heavenly liturgy and invites the assembled congregation to join in the acclamation of the heavenly choirs. The end of the Preface in particular has had a decisive influence on the iconography of the *Majestas Domini,* which was the point of departure for my remarks.[23] Compared to the biblical basis of the *Sanctus* in Isaiah 6, there are three new accents in the liturgical text.[24] The scene is no longer the Temple in Jerusalem, as in Isaiah, but heaven, which opens itself up to the earth in mystery.

For this reason it is no longer just the seraphim who are exulting, but all the hosts of heaven in whose acclamation the whole Church, redeemed humanity, can sing in unison because of Christ, who connects heaven and earth with each other. Finally, from there the *Sanctus* has been transferred from the "he"-form to the "you"-form: heaven and earth are full of your glory. The "Hosanna," originally a cry for help, thus becomes a song of praise. Whoever does not pay attention to the mystery character and cosmic character of the invitation to sing in unison with the praise of the heavenly choirs has already missed the point of the whole thing. This unison can occur in a variety of ways, and it always has to do with being representative of or standing in for others. The congregation assembled in one place opens into the whole. It also represents those who are absent and unites itself with those who are far and near. If the congregation has a choir that can draw it into cosmic praise and into the open expanse of heaven and earth more powerfully than its own stammering, then the representative function of the choir is at this moment particularly appropriate. Through the choir a greater transparency to the praise of the angels and therefore a more profound, interior joining in with their singing are bestowed than a congregation's own acclamation and song would be capable of doing in many places.

I suspect, though, that the real objection cannot consist of the acclamatory character or the *tutti*-demand; that would seem to me to be too shallow. Looming behind these is probably the fear that through a choral *Sanctus*, especially if it is also obligatory to connect it to the *Benedictus*, a kind of concert interlude and with that a pause in prayer would occur just at the start of the Eucharistic Prayer and so at a point where it is least justifiable. And indeed, this objection is correct—if one presupposes that there is neither the representative function of the choir nor an implicit singing and praying along with it in the outward silence of the congregation. If all those who are not singing during the *Sanctus* are only waiting for its end or can only focus themselves on a piece of religious music, then the performance by the choir is intolerable. But must this be the case? Have we not forgotten something here that we must urgently learn again? Perhaps it is helpful to remind the reader that the silent praying of the Canon by the priest did not arise because the singing of the *Sanctus* took so long that one had to start praying to save time.

The sequence of events is just the other way around. Certainly since Carolingian times, but perhaps even earlier, the priest has proceeded into the Canon "silently"; the Canon is the time of pure silence as "preparation for the nearness of God."[25] Briefly an "office of accompanying petitions, comparable to the oriental intercessions (*Ektenien*)" settled "on the celebrant's silent praying of the Canon like an exterior cover."[26] Later it was the singing of the choir that continued in this way, as Jungmann formulated it, "to retain the old dominating feature of the Eucharistic Prayer, thanksgiving and praise," and stretch it "over the entire Canon for the ears of the participants."[27] Even though we do not want to restore this state of affairs, it can still offer guidance for the way to go. Does it not do us good, before we set off into the center of the mystery, to encounter a short time of filled silence in which the choir calms us interiorly, leading each one of us into silent prayer and thus into a union that can occur only on the inside? Must we not relearn this silent, inner co-praying with each other and with the angels and saints, the living and the dead, and with Christ himself? This way the words of the Canon do not become worn-out expressions that we then in vain attempt to substitute with ever newly assembled phrases, phrases which conceal the absence of the real inner event of the liturgy, the departure from human speech into being touched by the eternal.

Lengeling's veto, which has been repeated by many others, is meaningless. The choral *Sanctus* has its justification even after the Second Vatican Council. But what about the *Benedictus*? The assertion that it may under no circumstances be separated from the *Sanctus* has been put so emphatically and with such apparent competence that only a few brave souls have been able to refuse to comply with it. But this assertion cannot be justified—neither historically, nor theologically nor liturgically. Of course it makes good sense to sing them together when a composition specifies this connection, which is ancient and very well founded. What has to be rejected here is again only the exclusion of their separation.

The *Sanctus* and *Benedictus* each have their own starting point in Scripture so that at first each one developed separately from the other. Whereas we find the *Sanctus* already in the first epistle of Clement (34:5–6)[28] and so definitely still in the apostolic age, we first encounter the *Benedictus*, as far as I can see, in the *Apostolic Constitutions*, that is, in the second half of the fourth century, and here as an acclamation before the distribution of Holy Communion, as a response to the phrase: "To the holy ones the Holy One." We find it again in the sixth century in Gaul, where it is connected to the *Sanctus*, as also happened in the tradition of the East.[29] Whereas the *Sanctus* evolved from Isaiah 6 and was then transferred from the earthly to the heavenly Jerusalem and so became the song of the Church, the *Benedictus* is based on a New Testament re-reading of Ps. 118:26. In the Old Testament text this verse is a blessing at the arrival of the festive procession in the temple; on Palm Sunday it received a new meaning, which, however, had already been prepared in the development of Jewish prayer, for the expression "he who comes" had become a name for the Messiah.[30] When the youths of Jerusalem shout this verse to Jesus, they are greeting him as the Messiah, as the king of the last days who enters the Holy City and the temple to seize possession of them. The *Sanctus* is ordered to the eternal glory of God; in contrast, the *Benedictus* refers to the advent of the incarnate God in our midst. Christ, the one who has come, is also always the one coming. His eucharistic coming, the anticipation of his hour, makes a present occurrence out of a promise and brings the future into the here and now. For this reason the *Benedictus* is meaningful both as an approach to the consecration and as an acclamation to the Lord who has become present in the eucharistic species. The great moment of his coming, the immensity of his real presence in the elements of the earth, definitely call for a response. The elevation, genuflection, and ringing of the bells are such faltering attempts at a reply.[31]

Following a parallel in the Byzantine rite, the reformers of the liturgy composed an acclamation of the people: "Christ has died, . . ." But the question of other possible acclamations to welcome the Lord who is coming/has come has been posed. It is evident to me that there is no more appropriate nor profounder acclamation, nor one that is more rooted in tradition than precisely this one: Blessed is he who comes in the name of the Lord. It is true that splitting the *Sanctus* and the *Benedictus* is not necessary, but it makes a lot of sense. If the choir sings the *Sanctus* and the *Benedictus* together, then the break between the Preface and the Eucharistic Prayer can indeed be too lengthy. When this happens, it no longer serves the congregation's silent, yet cooperative entering into cosmic praise because the inner tension is not sustained. On the other hand, if a filled silence and an interior greeting of the Lord along with the choir take place after the consecration event, it corresponds profoundly to the inner structure of the occasion.

The pedantic proscription of such a split, which came about not without reason in the development, should be forgotten as quickly as possible.

Now just a word about the *Agnus Dei*. In the Regensburg cathedral it has become a tradition that after the Sign of Peace the *Agnus Dei* is first spoken three times by both the priest and the people and then continued by the choir as a communion hymn during the distribution of Communion. Over against this custom it has been asserted that the *Agnus Dei* belongs to the rite of the breaking of the bread. Only a completely fossilized archaism can draw the conclusion from its original purpose of accompanying the time of the breaking of the bread that it should be sung exclusively at this point. As a matter of fact, it became a communion song as early as the ninth and tenth centuries when the old rites of the breaking the bread were no longer necessary because of the new hosts. J. A. Jungmann points out that in many cases in the early Middle Ages only one *Agnus Dei* was sung after the Sign of Peace while the second and third ones found their niche after Communion and thus accompanied the distribution of Communion where there was one.[32] And does the request for the mercy of Christ, the Lamb of God, not make sense at that exact moment when he defenselessly gives himself into our hands again as Lamb, the sacrificed, yet triumphant Lamb who holds the keys of history in his hands (Revelation 5)? And is the request for peace made to him, the defenseless yet victorious One, not appropriate especially at the moment of receiving Communion since peace was, after all, one of the names of the Eucharist in the early Church because it tears down the boundaries between heaven and earth and between peoples and states and joins humans to the unity of the Body of Christ?

At first glance, the Regensburg tradition and the conciliar as well as postconciliar reform seem to be two opposite worlds, which clash in harsh contradiction. Whoever stood right between them for three decades was able to experience the severity of the posed questions for himself. But where this tension is endured, it turns out that all this belongs to the stages of one single path. Only if one holds these stages together and holds out will they be correctly understood and will true reform flourish in the spirit of the Second Vatican Council—reform that is not discontinuity and destruction but purification and growth to a new maturation and a new fullness. The cathedral choirmaster who has borne the weight of this tension deserves thanks: This was not only a service for Regensburg and its cathedral, but a service for the entire Church.

NOTES

1. I have deliberately kept the local flavor of this address, held at a celebration for my brother, who was leaving the position of cathedral choirmaster, because it seems to me that it is precisely in the concrete case that the fundamentals can best be examined and clarified.

2. See H. Stampfer and H. Walder, *Die Krypta von Marienberg im Vinschgau* (Bozen, 1982).

3. Important for the theme of the *vita angelica* is J. Leclerq, *Wissenschaft und Gottverlangen* (Düsseldorf, 1963), p. 70; see also H. Stampfer and H. Walder, *Die Krypta*, p. 20.

4. H. Schützeichel, "Wohin soll ich mich wenden? Zur Situation der Kirchenmusik im deutschen Sprachraum," *Stimmen der Zeit* 209 (1991): 363–74.

5. Original text in Italian, *Acta Apostolicae Sedis* 36 (190): 329–39; German translation in *Dokumente zur Kirchenmusik unter besonderer Berücksichtigung des deutschen Sprachgebietes*, ed. H. B. Meyer and R. Pacik (Regensburg, 1981), pp. 23–34. One can find an implicit reference to Regensburg in the introduction, p. 24.

6. The introduction of the *motu proprio* (German translation, p. 25) and part II, 3 (German translation, pp. 27–28) explicitly speaks of the active participation of the faithful as a fundamental liturgical principle. G. Romanato portrays the past history of the *motu proprio* in his biography of Pius X, *Pio X: La vita di Papa Sarto* (Milan, 1992): In the seminary in Padua, Sarto had directed the *schola cantorum* and jotted down notes about this in a notebook he still carried with him as patriarch of Venice. As bishop of Mantua he had expended much time and energy on the *scuola di musica* during the reorganization of the seminary.

There he also met Lorenzo Perosi, who remained closely connected with him and who had received significant impulses for his path as church musician from his time of study in Regensburg. The relationship with Perosi continued in Venice. There Sarto published a pastoral letter in 1895 that was based on a memorandum he had sent to the Sacred Congregation of Rites in 1893 and which anticipates almost verbatim the *motu proprio* of 1913 (pp. 179ff.; pp. 213–14.; pp. 247–48; p. 330).

7. G. Romanato, *Pio X*, p. 247, also refers here to the judgment expressed by R. Aubert who has described Pius X as the greatest reformer of inner-ecclesial life since the Council of Trent.

8. See Schützeichel, "Wohin soll ich mich wenden?" (see n. 4), pp. 363–66.

9. CCC 1069.

10. Ibid., 1069, 1070.

11. Ibid., 1097, 1098.

12. See *Constitution on the Sacred Liturgy* 8; see also the following note.

13. CCC 1090; *Constitution on the Sacred Liturgy* 8. The *Catechism* points out that the same thought is also in the *Dogmatic Constitution on the Church* 50, last paragraph.

14. Ph. Harnoncourt, "Gesang und Musik im Gottesdienst," in *Die Messe: Ein kirchenmusikalisches Handbuch*, ed. H. Schützeichel (Düsseldorf, 1991), pp. 9–25 (quotation from p. 13).

15. Ibid., p. 17.

16. H. Schützeichel, "Wohin soll ich mich wenden?" (see n. 4), p. 366: "In principle every kind of music from Gregorian chant to jazz can be used in religious service. Naturally there is music that is more suitable and less suitable. The deciding factor is the quality."

17. Ph. Harnoncourt, "Gesang und Musik" (see n. 14), p. 24.

18. St. Cyprian, "De oratione dominica," 4, *CSEL* 3,1 (ed. Hartel), pp. 268–69 [translated into English from the German].

19. Ph. Harnoncourt, "Gesang und Musik" (see n. 14), p. 17.

20. See the thorough work by W. Menke, *Stellvertretung: Schlüsselbegriff christlichen Lebens und theologische Grundkategorie* (Einsiedeln and Freiburg, 1991).

21. Ph. Harnoncourt, "Gesang und Musik" (see n. 14), p. 21.

22. E. J. Lengeling, *Die neue Ordnung der Eucharistiefeier*, 2nd ed. (Regensburg, 1971), p. 234; see also B. Jeggle-Merz and H. Schützeichel, "Eucharistiefeier," in *Die Messe*, ed. H. Schützeichel (see n. 14), pp. 90–151, on this point, pp. 109–10.

23. See K. Onasch, *Kunst und Liturgie der Ostkirche* (Vienna, Cologne, and Graz, 1984), p. 329.

24. See J. A. Jungmann, *Missarum sollemnia* (Freiburg, 1952),

2:168ff. [Eng.: *The Mass of the Roman Rite* (New York, 1955) vol. 2].[25]
J. A. Jungmann, *Missarum sollemnia*, 2:174.

25. J. A. Jungmann, *Missarum sollemnia*, 2:174.

26. Ibid., pp. 175–76.

27. Ibid., p. 172.

28. See K. Onasch, *Kunst und Liturgie* (see n. 23), p. 329; J. A. Jungmann, *Missarum sollemnia* (see n. 24), 2:166. In Clement's epistle (*Ad Cor.* 34) we already find the connection of Isaiah 6 with Dan. 7:10, which is presupposed in the liturgical form of the *Sanctus*; it is precisely that version we found in the images of Marienberg: "Let us heed how the whole host of his angels stand by him." Concerning the dating of *1 Clement*, see Th. J. Herron, *The Dating of the First Epistle of Clement to the Corinthians* (Rome, 1988). Herron tries to show that *1 Clement* is not to be dated ca. A.D. 96, as is usually done, but rather around A.D. 70.

29. J. A. Jungmann, *Missarum sollemnia* (see n. 24), 2:170–71, nn. 41 and 42.

30. Ibid., p 171 n, 42; see also R. Pesch, *Das Markusevangelium* (Freiburg, 1977), 2:184.

31. See J. A. Jungmann, *Missarum sollemnia*, 2:165. In this context it might be of interest to note that the *motu proprio* of Pius X from 1903 (III 8, p. 29 of the German text; see n. 5) insisted that only liturgical texts were allowed to be used in the hymns at Mass; just *one* exception was permitted: following the custom of the Roman Church a motet could be sung after the *Benedictus* of a High Mass.

32. J. A. Jungmann, *Missarum sollemnia*, 2:413–22.

A Discussion between
F. Greiner and J. Ratzinger

❧

Question

The German Bishops' Conference of 1983 dealt with the theme of penance and reconciliation. On this occasion you published a document of the International Theological Commission on the same theme. Here it says: "In Jesus' preaching, the call to repentance is directly connected to the good news of the coming of the reign of God." Further on it states: "Therefore, when the Church in the imitation and in the mission of Jesus calls to repentance and proclaims the reconciliation of the world, it is proclaiming the God who is rich in mercy."

This call to repentance which the Church issues to each of us—is it an invitation to pursue a noble goal that we will never be able to achieve in time, or does it oblige us to obey with all the might and gifts of grace bestowed upon us?

Cardinal Ratzinger

Maybe we should speak of conversion [*Bekehrung*] instead of repentance [*Umkehr*], so that the simple and fundamental

truth that confronts us here in the New Testament will come
to light more clearly. My impression is that Christianity today
suffers to a great extent from a lack of readiness for conversion. People are eager to receive the comfort of religion; they
are also aware that they cannot give it to themselves, but that
it needs to be supported by the community of believers and
its authority. But they shrink from the binding nature of
Church teaching and Church life and reserve for themselves
the choice of what they consider to be religiously useful and
understandable. Committing oneself—that is, accepting the
whole package, including those elements which at the
moment do not seem to be either evident or useful—appears
as too large a step. The obligatory doctrines and life of the
Church are transposed into the invective "official Church"
and are thus declared to be something bureaucratic and
superficial. On the other hand, people are then surprised that
no energy for supporting life and the community issues from
the nonbinding Christianity of private choice.

In the Pentecost account of the Acts of the Apostles, Jesus'
call to conversion, to change one's ways, is concretized for the
situation following the resurrection. Through Peter's speech
the listeners realize that they killed the one whom God had
sent to them for their salvation. As the text says, they are cut
to the heart and ask: "What are we to do?" The answer is:
"Repent and be baptized, every one of you" (Acts 2:37–38)
The structure of conversion becomes very clear here. First of
all, it calls for hearing the apostolic message. Then it requires
deep shock in the face of one's own guilt; the "inability to
mourn"—or, better, the inability to be contrite—has to be
overcome, and in the awakening of one's conscience personal
guilt must turn into sorrow. Parenthetically I would like to
call to mind that the Church Fathers considered "insensitive-
ness," that is, the inability to mourn (to be contrite), to be the
real disease of the pagan world. As a matter of fact, without
deep shock in the face of one's own guilt there is no conversion. On the other hand, if there is no one there to shoulder

the guilt with them, to come to terms with it, and to forgive it, people *must* "harden their hearts," that is, deflect the realistic knowledge about themselves and their guilt. Hence, there is a reciprocity here, and everything hinges on it. Without looking at the Redeemer, who removes guilt by suffering, not by glossing it over, we cannot bear the truth about our own selves, and we escape into the first untruth, the blotting out of our own guilt, from which all further untruths and ultimately the general closure to truth ensue. Conversely, without the courage to be truthful with ourselves we can neither see nor believe the Redeemer. The Fathers therefore also described the basic act of conversion as "confession, speaking up" [*das Bekenntnis*], and this in two senses: confession of guilt as "doing the truth" and confession of the Redeemer Jesus Christ. It goes without saying that the act of conversion demands commitment, allegiance, and in this sense constancy, which is expressed in the bond with the apostolic words and with the sacrament of the Church, as the previously quoted speech of Peter indicates. The call to repentance does not mean tensely straining to seek first-rate moral performance all the time, but persisting in the sensitiveness to the truth and following him who makes the truth not only bearable but also fertile and salvific.

Question

The document of the International Theological Commission goes on to say: "The themes of penance and reconciliation affect the Church in her whole existence, in her teaching as well as in her life."

Can we conclude from this statement that the Church as she really exists in time and as a whole also has the obligation to repent, to become a new being (as it says in another place of the document), for instance in the sense of the phrase *Ecclesia semper reformanda* or even beyond it?

Cardinal Ratzinger

If I understand your question correctly, you are asking to what extent we can describe the Church herself as sinful. A further problem inextricably linked to this question is how radical reform in the Church can or even must be.

I think the Catholic tradition on this question is most concisely expressed in the prayer that the Roman liturgy places in the mouths of the priest and the faithful before they receive Communion. For the original meaning to come to light in its exact sense, we must bear in mind the old formulation as it was prayed before the reform of the liturgy. There it says: "Lord, . . . do not look upon *my* sins but upon the faith of *your* Church." It is important that the prayer was a prayer in the first person singular. One is not hiding in the nondescript mass of the "we" in which all have sinned (which is why no one needs to feel any particular personal responsibility). The one praying is meant personally: "*I* have sinned." This person must return to the act of conversion described above and sorrowfully recognize his or her guilt precisely at this great moment, when facing the Redeemer, who has become the Lamb of God. It is important that the Church, by making this a liturgical prayer, assumed that at every Eucharist those celebrating had reason to say such a thing. Up to the time of reform the prayer was first and foremost a prayer of the priest; the pope had to say it just as did the bishops, all the priests, and all the participants in the Eucharist. These words were definitely not intended for those distanced from the Church, for the excommunicated, or for those who in some other way were not living at the center of the faith community, but precisely for those who were preparing themselves for Communion. To receive Communion means to expose oneself to the fire of Christ's nearness and thus to the demand of conversion. In the Lord's Prayer all members of the Church without exception must say "forgive us our trespasses," but this communion prayer certainly did not imply that one could also call the

Church *as* Church sinful. Rather, it contrasted "my sins" with the "faith of your Church," which is the basis for my petition being heard.

This prayer, however, has become largely unintelligible today. Many priests therefore adapt it by saying, for example: Look not on the sins of your Church but on her faith. The personal sins have become the sins of the Church, while faith is looked upon as something personal: my way to say yes to God, which I will not let the Church dictate to me. In this inversion we see how far the common consciousness of Christians has distanced itself from the perspective of Catholic tradition. The inversion would be justified if the Church were assimilated into the collective body of the faithful. It is wrong if the Church as "body of Christ," as Christ's organism, is more than the sum of her empirical members. It should first of all be pointed out that the Church transcends the boundaries of death and includes the communion of saints. Furthermore it should be recalled that the ancient phrase *communio sanctorum* is not only to be translated as "communion *of* saints" but also as "communion in and with the holy." It thus refers to the indestructible gifts of the Church in Word, sacrament, and her basic sacramental structure, which have already come from the Lord. I do not want to explain this in more detail here; instead I would like to come back once more to the communion prayer. It qualified the Church with two predicates: she is "your" (the Lord's) Church and she is the bearer of "faith." Both are important to the same degree. The Church herself is not Christ, but a response to him, and this response is "faith." She is Church to the extent that she is an act of faith. And, from the opposite perspective, faith is by its very nature a believing with the Church; in the act of faith we become the Church and from her we actually receive this act. Since this is the case, she is "your Church" and not "our Church." Everything that is only "our" Church is not Church in the true sense of the word. Her nature is relation, turning toward the Lord, belonging to him (faith).

Something very practical follows from all this for your question. The "renewal" of the Church, which is always necessary, is not a matter of handcrafting structures as diligently as possible. All that emerges from this is homemade—"our" Church. What is made, however, is always of less value than the maker; a homemade Church can be interesting, but it cannot support us. What matters is not that we work as much as possible on the Church but that we let the "our" disappear as far as possible so that "his" Church, the Church herself, comes to light. This happens, however, to the extent that we "believe." Not making or doing, but believing renews the Church and us.

Question

The document of the International Theological Commission says that the sense of sin and guilt is in a state of crisis today. This is a result of the secularization in the Western world, but it is also a result of an administration of the sacraments in the Church which many Catholics experience as meaningless and empty. Do these two reasons concern only the recipients of the sacraments or also the administrators?

Cardinal Ratzinger

A few years ago Louis Bouyer put forward the thesis that the crisis in the Church today is in reality a crisis of the priests and members of religious orders. This is of course a very exaggerated statement, but it does indicate the focal point of the crisis correctly.

If this is the case, we have to ask: Why do those people seem to have the hardest time who, from the perspective of their mission and desire, should be inwardly one with the Church more than anyone else? I think we have not reflected on this question nearly enough up until now. To put it very generally, I see three main reasons for the crisis. The first is that those who themselves must proclaim the good news experience in a most dramatic way their alienation with regard to those things which our age chooses to regard as plausible. Theology takes common certitudes almost completely away from them. Splitting everything up into specializations lets individual issues stand out all too prominently without having developed a total view of what is Christian at all. The large contours of mystery disappear; it is so much more obvious to resort to new interpretations that impart a more modest yet more understandable and seemingly more realistic meaning to tradition. The second reason for the crisis is that the form of ecclesiastical office is alien to our society today: authority that is based not on consensus but on the representation of another who, as the voice of truth, has and is himself authority has become virtually incomprehensible today. It is very tempting to flee from such authority into the more proximate and simpler authority of administration by consensus. Finally, as the third reason there is the fact that the officeholder is also morally at the mercy of his surroundings, and he can easily grow tired of living his whole life-style in opposition to what is morally and amorally taken for granted in an epoch.

I am saying this to make it clear that the main problem should not be sought in the issue of a sacramental administration described as meaningless and empty. This is, by the way, once again a greater danger for the clergy than for the laity because there is nothing more perilous than getting used to what is magnificent, which humans would rather pull down to themselves than let themselves be pulled up to it. I feel increasingly uneasy when the earlier way of frequent confession is flippantly made out to be schematic, superficial, automatic, and therefore worthless. I also feel increasingly bitter about the vainglory that resounds when one emphasizes that confessions, although now reduced in number, have become so much more personal. In all too polished confessional dialogues a kind of coquetry and an industriousness to explain can easily arise which in the end hardly leave room for guilt at all. On the other hand, behind the mechanical nature of many an earlier confession lay a great inner seriousness that lacked an outward possibility for expression. Hidden in the clumsy forms were often an honesty and an intensity that can only merit our deep respect. It seems to me, therefore, that the most urgent problem of all is to help priests and members of religious orders attain an understanding of the reality "sacrament" again. What I said before about the flight from mystery into what is deemed plausible and from authority based on representation into administration by consensus has its most concrete expression here. In the sacraments the personal achievement of the officeholder does not matter, but that he retreat and make room for the other, the more magnificent One, so that "His Church" comes into being. Not only in the sacrament of penance is the temptation great to reduce the whole thing into a dialogue session that seems to be closer to people and more entertaining. One senses very quickly, however, that the true reality has been lost. We need a new education about the sacraments, which is where person and mystery encounter one another.

Question

The document of the International Theological Commission says: "The Church, in the imitation and mission of Jesus, calls to repentance." How does the Church do this? How does she do it before the world? Does she do it verbally or through exemplary, symbolic existence? How does she do it at a time when there is a reduced sense of God, sin, and redemption? What extraordinary means must the Church employ at such moments in history? Should she not constantly make it clear before the world that she is freeing all her energies for repentance, for a new being—and this not selectively or morally-ascetically but for the sake of a deepened participation in the life, suffering, and death of Jesus?

Cardinal Ratzinger

How does she do this? That is my question, too. To begin
with, we can and must recall the saying of Jesus that was
directed not only to his contemporaries: "This generation . . .
asks for a sign, but no sign will be given to it except the sign
of Jonah" (Luke 11:29; Matt. 12:39). What is this sign of
Jonah? For Nineveh it consisted simply of the prophet himself:
Coming from the distress of the shipwreck and marked by the
nearness of death and so by the power of God who is calling
him, he prophesies the impending doom of the city and calls
for penance at the same time. The sign of Jonah is then Jesus
Christ himself, who even as the raised One bears the wounds
of death and in this way holds out to the world the call for
repentance. In any case the sign of Jonah does not refer to
cleverly thought-out pastoral strategies. It refers to the witness
who has been shaken by faith and who communicates this
shock to the Ninevites of all times, telling them to their face in
no uncertain terms that they are heading for doom if they do
not do penance.

Nevertheless, these fundamental facts naturally do not free
us from searching with all our might for new possibilities to
make the sign of Jonah present today. No matter how good
all the strategies are, however, they are of no use if the
preacher himself does not first experience the shock and from
this find the courage to say the uncomfortable in a convinced
and convincing way.

Question

And yet the question remains about the ordinary and
extraordinary means for implementing the call to repentance
at this moment in time.

Cardinal Ratzinger

Without doubt. But a few things are also happening here;
just think of the Holy Year, the Pope's journeys, and the
Lenten projects each year that are constantly a trumpet blast

for reflection and action from the perspective of a new way of thinking. It is also important, by the way, that public forms of communal penance are being developed again. When Jonah came to Nineveh and demanded penance, everyone knew what penance was: one put on penitential clothes, fasted, and prayed. When Muslims celebrate Ramadan they know the procedure, and they also know that penance can become a concrete reality for a people only if it has a common form and a regular time in the course of a year. In our case penance has lost its communal form completely. When Christians are called upon to do penance, they do not know what this is; they may perhaps set up a committee or else depend totally on private views. The classical triad—fasting, praying, and giving alms—must be put back into its rightful place; Christians must also rediscover the ability for communal expression with which they publicly display their distance from all that is taken for granted in the world.

In the liturgical sphere there are diverse efforts to lower the "threshold" before the confessional, as Bishop Averkamp put it at the synod of bishops. There is personal confession and spiritual counsel in dialogue form; there is the penitential service as a way of collective examination of conscience and communal preparation for individual confession. The Stations of the Cross, praying the sorrowful mysteries of the rosary, and Mount of Olives devotions were also "penitential services" with a strong christological emphasis. The encounter with the suffering Christ was supposed to evoke that "ability to mourn" which leads people inwardly to the path of penance. I believe it is completely possible to revive these classical ways of encounter with the passion of Christ and thus with the truth of one's own guilt as well as with the grace of forgiveness. I think it is good that we are seeking and finding new forms for this. The early Church also offered her believers a rich variety of penitential forms: Origen names seven of them in a profound text in his commentary on Leviticus.[1] But of course the form should not be the sum total of it.

For example, when the penitential rite of the Mass was replaced by a wildly applauded ballet-pantomime at the Catholic Congress in Munich in 1984, a spectacle took the place of penance for which those present applauded one another. It is hardly possible to distance oneself further from what is meant by an act of penance.

It has just occurred to me that Romano Guardini entitled what is probably his most important work on liturgical renewal *Besinnung vor der Feier der heiligen Messe* [*Meditation before the Celebration of Mass*]; he called another important work *Liturgische Bildung* [*Liturgical Formation*]. People today are frequently trying to "shape" or "structure" the liturgy in such a way that there is no longer a need for meditation beforehand or any liturgical formation because they want to give it the most superficial form of intelligibility. A return to the original spirit of liturgical renewal is imperative. We do not need new forms through which we wander off further and further into what is only superficial; we need formation and meditation—that kind of spiritual deepening without which all celebrating remains fleeting superficiality.

Question

A focal point of the discussion at the bishops' synod on penance and reconciliation was the question of whether general absolution should not become an ordinary, equally valid form of sacramental penance along with individual confession, until now the only binding form. The bishops came out against this and appealed for the continuing validity of the norms that were formulated after the Council and have since been adopted in the new Code of Canon Law. These permit general absolution only in rigidly defined, exceptional situations and demand in addition that individual confession follow as soon as possible. It cannot be denied (and you yourself have described it so) that since the First World War, whose mass battles were the occasion for the granting of general absolution to those threatened by death, the Church slowly drew conclusions from this unique situation and gradually learned to expand the concept of emergency which at the start had governed a very narrowly defined meaning. Why should this development not continue? Could general absolution not truly become a new form for introducing many to penance? Could it not lead them in a special way to the social dimension of sin and to the communal moment that lies in absolution, which is always—as Augustine has emphatically brought out—backed up by the prayer and support of the whole Church, which accompanies and sustains the sinners in their penance?

Cardinal Ratzinger

First we must realize that the Church cannot do everything she thinks might be useful. We must again make ourselves aware of how terrifying it really is when a person dares to say: I absolve you from your sins. No one can say this on his own authority; if he does so, it is blasphemous as well as inconsequential. When you read the New Testament, you see that extreme agitation arises wherever Jesus claims the right to forgive sins. "Who but God alone can forgive sins?" the scribes ask in the story of the paralytic whose friends let him down through the roof and lay him at Jesus' feet (Mark 2:3–7). Jesus is in agreement with his opponents on this point; the purpose of the forgiveness of sins is precisely to lead them to the realization that the living God himself is speaking and acting in Jesus, as he then illustrates through the physical healing of the one suffering. Nor can the Church forgive sins on her own. The "I" of the "I forgive" is the I of the Lord himself. One cannot appropriate this I as one likes, but only tremulously make use of it in the precise manner in which the Lord has entrusted it to us.

For this reason the controversy surrounding the Council of Trent that came up in this context is based on a false formulation of the question. In canons 6 and 7 of its decree on penance (DS 1706 and 1707), the Council of Trent decided that individual confession, in which the penitent confesses each of the mortal sins that have been discerned as such after conscientious preparation, is necessary according to "divine law." In the sixteenth century, however, the phrase "divine law" had a much broader range of meaning than we sense in this expression today. The discussion at present thus amounts to asking if, according to a possible usage of the time, "divine law" does not indeed mean Church law here, which could then of course be changed. But one can show from the Council records with sufficient clarity that for the core of their statement—individual confession is the prerequisite for absolution—the Fathers wanted to avert just such an extension of the idea of divine law. Otherwise they would have simply been confirming the theses of the Reformation that they were opposing. In this context I think the observation is also important that an old conciliar tradition of the East was adopted here almost word for word. The so-called *Concilium Quinisextum* (692), an addendum to the Third Council of Constantinople, which counts as an ecumenical council in the Orthodox Church, states in canon 102 that to gain absolution it is necessary to make the sins visible according to their nature and to see in the sinner a readiness to change. The canons of this Church council belong to the fundamentals of Orthodox Church life; it therefore becomes clear that Trent promulgated truly "ecumenical" ordinances, common traditions of East and West.

Above all, one is on the wrong track if the impression is given that the burden of proof lies with those who see the limit of Church authority. The opposite is the case. It is not the limit of authority that must be proved; the burden of proof lies with the person who ascribes new powers to the Church which she did not know before. Whoever maintains that the Church also can collectively forgive sins as she likes must show where this right comes from. This person must do so with the timidity and awe of one who knows what an outrage it would be if the Church claimed to be speaking in the name of the Lord but spoke only in her own name. Until now no one has offered proof for such a prerogative of the Church, and no one can offer it now either. The Church cannot say "I absolve *all of you*"; she can only say in response to a personal confession "I absolve *you*"—that is, one individual. She must keep to this humility.

This alone also corresponds to the structure of all the sacraments: no sacrament is administered collectively to a group. You cannot sprinkle a crowd of people with water or dunk them in water and say over them: "I baptize you all." You can only say: "I baptize you"—that is, this one person. The same is true for all the other sacraments. Besides, this sacramental structure is what each individual needs today: everyone stands before God not as part of a group but with his or her own name. God calls each person in this way. Precisely in this way each person becomes capable of communion, which either grows from individuals or declines where people become replaceable parts of a collective group.

Question

But it is still true that the sacrament of penance has gone through massive changes in its history, so that at first glance one can hardly recognize the identity of the one sacrament at all. Does this not relativize considerably the form of the sacrament of penance familiar to us? Why should further developments not be possible as well?

Cardinal Ratzinger

Further developments are of course possible. The new forms mentioned above—individual confession with spiritual counsel in the form of dialogue and communal preparation for penance followed by individual confession—are indeed proof of this. The one form aims at an even more individual structuring of penance, the other at a stronger communal orientation in the penitential event. Various emphases still remain possible that can then create appropriate expressions for themselves. Furthermore, with respect to these two aspects there are not only variables in the history of penance but also constants, and over and above that an underlying direction in the development. It stretches from the Church's great timidity in claiming the authority to forgive sins to an ever greater expansion of its use. At the beginning there was only the single forgiveness of sins and the question of whether it could refer to all sins. First it became clear that no sin is excluded from forgiveness and then that forgiveness can be repeated as long as and as often as the "ability to mourn" and to begin anew persist.

Furthermore, it seems to me that a new, impartial analysis of the first centuries of the history of penance is imperative. The current view was shaped entirely by the research of the prominent historian of dogma Bernhard Poschmann from Breslau, whose views Karl Rahner adopted and imprinted upon our theological consciousness. In the meantime Poschmann's differentiated positions have become simplified to the notion that initially there was only public penance attended by the community and that Irish monasticism invented "private confession" only later. Today we know that in early Judaism at the time of Jesus the confession of sins by the individual—that is, personal confession—was a common practice which continued and merged organically into the life of the Christian communities. I will mention only a few examples. Baptism by John was connected to confession, to an acknowledgment of sins by the person to be baptized (Mark 1:5; Matt. 3:6). The Letter of James presupposes that the faithful practice the mutual confession of sins before each other and probably also a confession of sins before the presbyters within the framework of the anointing of the sick (5:16).[2] The Acts of the Apostles (19:18) speaks of a confession of sins by those who had become believers. The *Didache* (a treatise written presumedly in Syria at the beginning of the second century) requires a confession of sins, which can definitely not be thought of as reduced to collective forms, before the celebration of the Eucharist (14:1). One must be careful in classifying the confessions of sins mentioned here with the sacrament of penance in the true sense. But together with the processes of excommunication, as they occur, for example, in the letters of Paul, they belong to the elements from which it was possible to form the structure of the sacrament. The practice of personal confession could obviously not be kept up in the growing Gentile-Christian communities and was reduced to general formulae. But the monasticism that was evolving in the early Church took up this practice and also made it available again to the rest of the faithful. Only in this way can we understand how personal confession, falsely called "private confession," already became the normal form of penance at the close of Christian antiquity in the Eastern Church, which had experienced no influence from Ireland. In 692 the basic structure of this rite could then be defined in a conciliar canon in the East.

We do not yet know in detail how this monastic tradition, which then rapidly became the general church tradition of the East, found its way into the West. But in 589 the Third Council of Toledo, trying to turn back the clock, once again wanted to forbid this penitential form in Spain, which it took for granted as the form of the sacrament already dominating by that time. That again points to quite a stretch of history in the West which must have preceded this. Only about half a century later personal confession was unanimously approved by the bishops gathered at the synod in Chalons-sur-Saône (644–656). This again illustrates that it had already found a home in Gaul. It is undisputed that the history-making Irish penitential books are based on old traditions of the Orthodox Church. It seems to me to be significant that the best-known book was written by a Greek, Archbishop Theodore of Canterbury (died in 690). All this shows that Ireland did not create something new. Rather, the old tradition of monasticism and the Orthodox Church, which for its part was based on the tradition of Judeo-Christianity and the apostolic period, returned from Ireland to the continent. In contrast, it proved to be a mistaken sort of conservatism when the Franconian reform councils of the ninth century tried to reestablish the solemn form of the old rite of public penance. It was also a one-sided romanticism that was neither theologically nor historically justified when some in the circles of theological and liturgical reform before and after the Second Vatican Council tried to orient themselves based on this model, which in reality had almost suffocated the early Church. Faced with the discrepancy between the unrepeatability of penance and the repeatability of sin and human weakness, people had largely resigned themselves to postponing baptism until the hour of death. The Church was quite literally in danger of becoming a dying Church. It is absurd to appeal to this form today and then to change it to a penintential celebration with general absolution when personal public confession at the beginning and the unrepeatability of absolution at the end were its essential characteristics. In contrast, history shows unequivocally that only the form of individual and frequent confession developed in monasticism on the basis of the Judeo-Christian tradition has proved itself capable of surviving in the long run. The practice of this form, given to all Christians as sinners, also makes it possible for each and every one of them to cross the threshold to confession and penance. The converse must also be stated: this form alone gives the Church vitality. No other form has been able to assert itself for any length of time. There are, on the one hand, anthropological reasons for the fact that, in terms of its fundamental structure, it is a common possession of East and West in spite of all the differences in the concrete rite. On the other hand, this fact also points to the genesis of this form from the common ground of biblical tradition.

As a matter of fact, only in this way is it possible to achieve the correct balance between the personal and the social factors in penance. It seems to me that the proponents of general absolution turn this relationship upside down: that which should actually be personal—confession and absolution—is made communal. That which requires a communal form—the penitential life-style and the implementation of conversion in one's life—is consigned to one's personal point of view. In this scenario, however, the Christian form of life develops and the Christian transformation of the world takes place but repentance does not penetrate the social dimensions. Today we need exactly the opposite of such attempts, namely, that radical personal responsibility to which personal confession corresponds. On the other hand, we need public and communal ways of living in which Christians accept the need for conversion and in this way try to give the world a different face.

Question

On the one hand, we hold on to the requirement of repentance and apply it to both the individual believer and the whole Church in such a way that this repentance becomes clear to the world and the symbolic nature of the Church is unambiguous. On the other hand, the Pauline postulate remains valid: Be all things to all people (that is, do not be an elite counterworld, countersociety, or sect), which of course can be and perhaps must be understood as conforming. Can both claims be fulfilled in the life of the Church and in the life of the individual, or are there not certain paradoxical features attached to this dual demand?

Cardinal Ratzinger

Of course there are paradoxical aspects here. But we must not forget that the Pauline demand to conform should be defined in the light of its goal; it is quite clearly interpreted by the figure of the apostle himself. As far as cultural and sociological styles are concerned, Paul is open-minded. But he is inexorably resolute where the core of the gospel message is at stake. The Letter to the Galatians demonstrates this most clearly, but it is also quite obvious in all the other letters. It is not possible to draw up a theoretical formula for the correct balance between the sympathetic response to people in accordance with the gospel and unflagging faithfulness to the Lord. The balance will be discovered all the more automatically the deeper people are grounded in the yes of their faith in Christ, the deeper they have "put on" Christ, as Paul expressed it. They then stand in an inner communion of discernment with Christ. Faith has become personal and is no longer a set of statements for which we must try to find the proper place in daily life. From the inside, faith itself shows the way and points out what believers must not give up if they do not want to betray themselves *and* others; at the same time it leads them to the others, gives them that love for the other which opens up paths of understanding. The paradox solves itself in the union with the One who is the way.

NOTES

1. Origen, "Homiliae in Leviticum," 2, *GCS* 29:295, 6–297, 27.
2. See F. Mussner, *Der Jakobusbrief* (Freiburg, 1975), p. 225.

10

Preparation for Priestly Ministry

❧

A draft on renewed formation for priestly ministry was also part of the extensive reform concept of the Second Vatican Council.[1] But the late 1960s, when the program was supposed to go into effect, were marked in the entire Western world by the outbreak of a crisis in its spiritual foundations that had been smoldering for a long time. In the view of the Council, renewal included to the same degree continuity and change. But in the revolutionary climate of those years only change appeared as hope; everything that had been handed down from the past counted simply as ballast, as a fetter and a threat from which we had to free ourselves at long last. As a result, the time of renewal initially turned into a crisis. The question was whether the seminary made any sense at all; even the goal of its education, the priesthood, seemed to many to be a misunderstanding of the New Testament and a relapse into the old and the past, which should be overcome once and for all. Since then, the first fuss has abated. It is again becoming apparent that people can live only facing forward and can go further only if they are standing in a context. Growth is possible only where there are roots, and new insight can flourish only if we have not lost our memory. One cannot dismiss historical remembering, which is the intention and purpose of anniversaries, as romantic nostalgia; it is fertile when it becomes a reflection on what perdures and at the same time a search for a way that leads forward.

LET YOURSELF BE BUILT INTO A SPIRITUAL HOUSE: FORMATION INTO THE FAMILY OF GOD

When I was appointed archbishop of Munich and Freising in 1977, I found myself thrown right into the midst of this situation of crisis and turmoil. The number of seminarians in the archdiocese had decreased; they lived as guests in the ducal Georgianum, which Duke George the Rich had founded in 1494 as the Bavarian regional seminary at the University of Ingolstadt, which itself was later moved to Munich. I knew from the very beginning that it was my most pressing duty to give the diocese its own seminary again, even though many doubted that such an undertaking made any sense in the changed Church. Shortly before I had to leave my home diocese again, on November 20, 1981—the feast of the diocesan patron, St. Korbinian, which also happened to be a day shrouded by rain—I had the pleasure of laying the cornerstone for the seminary building, which was already towering in an impressive way. Thus, I could at least cement a beginning which had to go on.

As I pondered what should be written on the stone, I came across the wonderful verses from the First Letter of Peter in which Israel's titles of honor were applied to the people who had been baptized: "Like living stones let yourselves be built into a spiritual house, to be a holy priesthood, to offer spiritual sacrifices acceptable to God through Jesus Christ" (1 Pet. 2:5). These verses are probably part of a New Testament baptismal catechesis. They apply the theology of the covenant and election with which the Sinai event was interpreted in the Old Testament to the new community of Jesus Christ. It is thus shown here in simple terms what it means to be a baptized person and how church, God's living house, grows in this world. But what nobler and better thing could actually happen in a seminary than that young men completely grow into the call of baptism and into the call of being disciples and totally become a living Church? It therefore seemed to me that St. Peter's address to the baptized says everything essential about seminary life; it may rightly be regarded as a programmatic slogan and as the cornerstone of such a house.

What is the purpose of a seminary? How should priestly formation take place today? To begin with, in our scriptural passage we find the phrase about being built into a spiritual house from living stones. Generally speaking, "house" in the biblical sense does not denote the stone building as much as kinship or family—a usage that lives on in our time when, for example, we speak of the House of Wittelsbach, the House of Habsburg, and so on.[2] The baptized, originally strangers to each other, are to become one family, the family of God. This process should happen concretely in the seminary, so that the future priest will then be able to bring people together into the family, into the household of God in his parish or wherever he may be. But there is still the word "spiritual" in connection with house. This does not mean, as our sense of language suggests, a house that is only metaphorical, figurative, or unreal. The word "spiritual" here comes from Holy Spirit, that is, from the creative power without which nothing would be real at all. A spiritual house, one built by the Holy Spirit, is therefore truly the real house. The togetherness that derives from the Holy Spirit goes deeper and is stronger and more alive than a mere blood relationship. People brought together because they have been jointly touched by the Holy Spirit are closer to each other than people in any other relationship. It is in this context that John's Gospel speaks of those who believed in the name of the Logos and have thus received a new origin, "who were born, not of blood or of the will of the flesh or of the will of man, but of God" (1:13). Here John establishes the connection with the One who was born not by human choice but through the power of the Holy Spirit: Jesus Christ. We become a "spiritual house" when we are a house, a family unit or domestic communion with Jesus Christ. This bestows that inner harmony, that new identification and that new foundation of life which are stronger than all natural differences and make true inner relationship grow. The seminary, like the Church and like every family, is constantly under construction. It emerges as a whole again and again only when people let themselves be built into a living house through the encounter with Jesus Christ.

We could now say quite simply that the seminary's essential task is to provide space in which this spiritual constructing can always recur. Its purpose is to be a place of encounter with Jesus Christ which binds people to him in such a way that they are able to become his voice in the present, his voice for the people and the world of today. This fundamental statement becomes more concrete if we return once again to our text. The goal is the house; what precedes it are the stones—living stones in the case of a living house. The fact that our verse talks about building in the passive voice is part of this: Like living stones, let yourselves be built into a spiritual house. Our thirst for action requires that we translate such words without exception into the active voice: Let us build the kingdom of God, the Church, a new society, and so forth. The New Testament sees our role differently. The construction manager is God or the Holy Spirit. We are the stones—for us building means being built. An old liturgical hymn for the consecration of a church describes this graphically; it speaks of the blows of the curative chisel, the thorough treatment with the master's hammer, and the right assembly of the pieces through which the blocks of stone finally grow together into the great building of the new Jerusalem. This touches on something very important: build-

ing means to be built. If we want to become a house, we—
each and every one of us—must accept the fate of being cut
and carved. In order to be suitable for the house we must let
ourselves be bent into shape for the places where we are
needed. Those who want to be stones in and for the whole
must let themselves be bound to the whole. They can no
longer just do whatever comes to mind and seems worthwhile. They can no longer just go wherever they want. They
must accept that their belt will be fastened by another and
that they will also be led where they do not want to go (see
John 21:18). In John's Gospel we find yet another image for
this—the vine that is to bear fruit must be pruned; it must let
itself be cut. Only the pain of being pruned produces a greater
harvest (John 15:2).

Priestly formation must provide more than formation or
education for the right way of being human. First, it belongs
to priestly formation to learn the virtues thoroughly without
which no family can stay together for long. This is of particular importance to the priest: not only must he be capable of
living with others in the family of the rectory, the parish, and
the whole Church; it is also his duty to bring and hold people
together in the communion of faith, people who are strangers
to each other in terms of their origin, education, disposition,
and living conditions. He must guide people so that they
become capable of reconciliation, forgiving and forgetting,
endurance and generosity. He must help them to tolerate others in their otherness, to have patience with others, to exhibit
trust, prudence, discretion, and openness to the right degree,
and to do still a lot more. Above all, he must be capable of
standing by people in their pain—in physical suffering as well
as in all the disappointments, debasements, and fears that no
one can escape. How can he do this if he himself has not
learned the lesson beforehand? The ability to accept and
weather suffering is a fundamental condition for succeeding
as a human being. Where it is never learned, existence is
doomed to failure. Being up-in-arms about everyone and

everything contaminates the ground of the soul, so to speak, and turns it into barren land. The priest must learn how to cope with pain—formerly one spoke of asceticism in this context. No one likes this word any longer; it becomes more palatable when we translate it from Greek into English—training. Everyone knows that without training and the willpower that goes with it there is no success. Nowadays one trains for all kinds of skills with enthusiasm and persistence, and in this way record performances in many areas are possible that were once deemed inconceivable. But why does it seem so outlandish to train for real life, for the right life—to practice the arts of denial, of self-control, and of freeing ourselves from our addictions?

Passion for the Truth

From the many points that could be mentioned here, I would like to emphasize just one in particular: educating people to the truth, to be truthful. People are often uncomfortable with the truth; it is probably the best guide to selflessness and true freedom. Let us take the example of Pilate. He knows very well that this accused Jesus is innocent and that according to the law he should acquit him. He wants to do this, too. But then this truth comes into conflict with his position; it threatens to cause him trouble or even the loss of his job. Unrest could occur; he could appear in an unfavorable light before the emperor, and so on. So he chooses rather to sacrifice the truth, which does not scream or defend itself, even though its betrayal leaves him with a dull sense of failure. This situation is repeated in history again and again. Let us recall just one positive example: Thomas More. How natural it appeared to concede supremacy over the Church to the king! There was no explicit dogma that clearly forbade this. All the bishops had already done it—why should he, the layman, risk his life and cast his family into ruin? Even if he did not want to save his own neck, ought he not, when considering the hierarchy of values, at least give his family priority over his stubborn insistence on his conscience? Such cases show macroscopically, so to speak, what happens again and again in our lives in miniature. I could get myself out of trouble if I made a small concession to the untruth. Or the other way around: accepting the consequences of the truth would cause me immense trouble. How often does that happen? And how often do we fail! The situation Thomas More had to face is constantly present when translated into everyday life. Lots of people say that, so why shouldn't I as well? Why should I disturb the peace of the group? Why should I make a fool of myself? Isn't the peace of the community more important than my know-it-all attitude? As a result, group conformity turns into a tyranny opposing the truth. Georges Bernanos, who was haunted by the mystery of the priestly vocation and the tragedies of its failure, dramatically portrayed this danger in the character of Bishop Espelette. This popular bishop had been an academic; he is educated and kind and always knows how to say just what fits the situation and what the educated expect from a bishop in this position. "The courage of this shrewd priest, however, deceives no one but himself. His intellectual cowardice is immense. . . . No one is less lovable than one who only lives to be loved. Such souls, so clever as to change according to the taste of each and every one, are only mirrors." In his analysis Bernanos gets to the bottom of this failure: "'I belong to my times' he repeats, and this with the expression of a man who is testifying on behalf of himself. . . . But he has never taken into account that each time he says this he denies the eternal character which was imprinted on him."[3]

I do not hesitate to claim that the lack of truth is the major disease of our age. Success and results have outstripped the truth everywhere. Renouncing the truth and escaping into group conformity are only apparently a way to peace. Such types of communion are built on sand. The pain of truth is the condition for real communion. It has to be accepted day in and day out. Only in truth's humble patience do we mature from the inside and become free from ourselves and for God.

This is the point at which the metaphor of the living stones appears again. Peter explains the inner claim of the metaphor with Ps. 118:22, which had long since become a basic chris- tological text: "The stone which the builders rejected has become the cornerstone." We will not investigate in detail the theology of death and resurrection that is concealed in this verse. But working with the idea of living stones did at least lead us to the insight that building includes being built, that building cannot take place without the passive, the passion of purification. Bernanos described pain as the essence of the divine heart, and physical and spiritual suffering as the most precious thing the Lord inflicts on us.[4] The rejected stone is the metaphor for the Lord, who has taken the deadly pain of radical love upon himself and thus become a place for all of us—a cornerstone that makes a living house, a new family out of torn humanity. In the seminary, in the training of priests we are not simply building some group or other. There would then be the danger that the pain of being fit into the building is aimed only at group conformity and that in the process we sacrifice our truth. We are not building according to a self-made norm. We are letting ourselves be made into a building by him who is the prototype and final image of all of us—by the second Adam, whom Paul calls a life-giving spirit (1 Cor. 15:45). This building plan justifies the tribulation of the purifications and guarantees that these are purifications, not demolitions. We grow into this building by trying to learn "whatever is true, whatever is honorable, whatever is just, whatever is pure, whatever is pleasing, whatever is com- mendable, if there is any excellence and if there is anything worthy of praise" (Phil. 4:8). We are right for this building if we are truthful.

Where this goal is operative, a seminary becomes a home. Without this common path it would be only a juxtaposition of student rooms whose inhabitants would remain alone, each in the end by himself. Precisely the willingness to be purified guarantees the humor and the cheerfulness of such a house. Where it is lacking, grumbling and being fed up with everything and oneself reign. In this climate the days are gray and joy does not thrive because it does not find the sun that it needs for its growth.

HOUSE AND TEMPLE
SERVING THE WORD WHICH BECAME FLESH

These reflections open up an approach to a second step, in which, beyond the essential education of humans and Christians, we can speak about formation for the priest's vocation in particular. The saying [in 1 Pet. 2:5] about the spiritual house of living stones once again provides our starting point. This is the house God builds in the world, which we at the same time build for him—the "house of God." Thus, the whole theology of the temple is included in this phrase. The temple is first of all the dwelling place of God, the place of his presence in this world. For this reason it is the place of gathering in which the covenant is effected ever anew. It is a place of God's encounter with his people, and the people also finds itself in it. The temple is the place from which God's word goes out, the site where the standard of his instruction is set up and becomes visible over a long distance. And so it is ultimately the site of God's glory. This appears in the inviolable purity of his words. This appears also, however, in the festive beauty of ritual action. The glory shows itself in glorification, which is the response to the call of God's words—a concentrated and anticipated response that must be continued in the conduct of one's whole life, which is supposed to become an echo of God's glory. The tearing of the temple curtain at the moment of Jesus' death on the cross signified that this building had ceased to be the place of encounter for God and humans in this world. From the moment of Jesus' death his body, which was given up for us, is the new and true temple. The external destruction of the stone temple in the year 70 only makes visible for all of history what already happened in the death of Jesus.[5] The following psalm verse has now come into full force: "Sacrifice and offering you do not desire, but a body you prepared for me" (Ps. 40:6; Heb. 10:5). Ritual has now gained its new and final meaning: we glorify God by becoming one body with Christ, that is, a new spiritual existence in which he embraces us completely, with life and limb (see 1 Cor. 6:17). We glorify God by letting ourselves be pulled into that act of love which was fulfilled on the cross. Glorification and covenant, worship and life become inseparably one. Jesus' hour, which lasts until the end of time, consists in his being on the cross and drawing us to himself (John 12:32) so that we may all become "one" with him (Gal. 3:28).

The essential elements that defined the Old Testament cult continue to be valid in the new cult, which is performed continually in our paschal transition from ourselves into the place of the body of Christ. These elements, however, only now acquire their full meaning. "Temple," as we said, is first of all a place for God's word. Since the priesthood serves the incarnate Word, it must make God's word present in its flawless purity and abiding relevance. It is essential for the priest of the New Covenant that he not expound merely some private philosophy of life that he has concocted for himself or pieced together from other sources; rather, he is to express the words that were entrusted to our safe keeping and which we may not water down, as Paul puts it in a drastic and vivid way in the Second Letter to the Corinthians (2 Cor. 2:17). Here we are confronted with the challenging demand that the priest must take on; behind this the entire breadth and depth of what it means to form and train priests becomes visible. As a priest I am not allowed to express my private views; I am the ambassador of another, and this alone makes my message important. "So we are ambassadors for Christ, since God is making his appeal through us; we entreat you on behalf of Christ, be reconciled to God" (2 Cor. 5:20). These words of

Paul remain the valid definition of the basic form and fundamental mission of priestly existence in the Church of the New
Covenant. I have to deliver the message of another, and this
means first of all that I must know what it is, I have to have
understood it, and I have to make it my own.

This proclamation, however, requires more than merely the
posture of a telegram messenger who passes on foreign words
faithfully without being affected by them in any way. Instead,
I must pass on the words of another in the first person and in
a very personal way, and I must commit myself to them in
such a way that they become my words entirely. For these
words require not a telex operator but a witness. Whereas
people usually get an idea and then look for words to express
it, the process here is the other way around: the words precede
them. People put themselves at the disposal of the words and
hand themselves over to the words. The essence of each and
every priestly formation involves this process of getting to
know, understanding, and entering into or immersing oneself
in these words. In his book on retreats, Father Kolvenbach
calls this subordination of one's own understanding to Church
teaching a *sacrificium intellectus*; he goes on to say:

> This *sacrificium* marks the entire intellectual activity . . . as a
> sacrifice in the true sense of the word and thus stamps it as
> priestly. . . . The ability . . . to preach does not first and fore-
> most depend . . . on knowledge, but on the priest's personally
> entering into the body of Christ and on our understanding's
> entering into God's word which has been passed down to us.
> Just as for the Levites, prophets, and apostles, the never-end-
> ing learning process for the preacher of God's word consists in
> placing God's glory above everything else. . . . A priest must
> devote himself totally to the word of God."[6]

From this Father Kolvenbach explains the mysterious Pauline
expression that we must "put on Christ": putting on Christ
involves this process of identifying ourselves with the words of
faith and immersing ourselves in these words so that they
become our own words because we have become part of them.

Practically speaking this means that in the study of theology the intellectual and spiritual dimensions are inseparable from each other. The fact that God's words, something that God has said and is saying to us, are accessible in the world is truly the most exciting news I can imagine at all. Only we are too dulled through everyday use to grasp the awesomeness of this statement. I became newly aware of this through an anecdote that Helmut Thielicke tells in his memoirs. Two philology students who had never had any kind of religious instruction attended one of his sermons in the Hamburg Michel [St. Michael's Church in Hamburg]. What impressed them most was the Our Father prayed together at the end, whose text they had never heard before. Since everyone seemed to know it, they did not dare ask about it but went on a search for it themselves. Their attempt to find it in the public library failed. They could not find the text in the library of the school of theology either. The matter became ever more baffling until they finally hit upon the idea to write down the Our Father as it was being prayed during the religious service on the radio on Sunday morning. Their account to Thielicke about their long and difficult expedition in search of the Lord's Prayer—which, by the way, ultimately led to their conversion to the Catholic Church—closed: "Thus we finally had a copy of the Our Father in the bag."[7] What the Lord had to acknowledge concerning the faith of the pagans is repeated here in our own time: "Truly I tell you, in no one in Israel have I found such faith" (Matt. 8:10). To apprehend the adventure of the nearness of God's word in all its breathtaking beauty and to get involved in it with body and soul belongs to the essence of a priest's vocation. For this reason we should spare no effort in discerning God's words. If it is worthwhile to learn Italian to read Dante in the original, then it must be all the more obvious to us that we should learn to read the Scriptures in the original languages as well. The utmost care typical of historical studies is of course part of our expedition into the word of God. Rational discipline, the discipline of methodical work, is an indispensable component of the path to the priesthood. Whoever loves wants to know. You cannot know enough about the one you love. The carefulness of discernment is therefore an inner demand of love. Incidentally, methodical discipline, which constantly wrests favorite ideas from us for the sake of obedience to what is already given, is an irreplaceable way of educating us to truth and truthfulness. It is an essential part of that selflessness shown by witnesses who do not proclaim themselves but place themselves in the service of something greater. A piety that chooses to skip this turns into religious fanaticism. Edification without truth is a kind of spiritual self-gratification to which we must not fall prey.

A careful and disciplined effort to understand Holy Scripture is the basis of education to the priesthood. But of course a mere historical reading of the Bible is not enough. We do not read it as the former words of humans; we read it as the word of God always present in a new way that was given to all ages through the people of a past age. To lodge this word solely in the past means to deny the Bible as Bible. In fact, such a merely historical interpretation, which focuses only on the past, leads with inner necessity to the denial of the canon and therefore to dismissing the Bible as Bible. Accepting the canon has always meant reading the words in a way that transcends their moment in time; it means understanding the people of God as the abiding bearer of the word and author in the authors. Since no people is the people of God by its own doing, accepting it as subject simultaneously means acknowledging God in and through this subject as the one who actually inspires its path and its recorded memory. Exegesis becomes biblical exegesis and theology by placing itself in this perspective; theology comes into being because there is the common subject, the Church. Without this subject it does not exist at all.[8] Wherever theology ignores this subject it turns into a philosophy of religion. The set course of theological studies disintegrates into a juxtaposition of historical, philosophical, and praxeological disciplines in the same way the canon itself disintegrates if there is not an abiding subject which alone can accept responsibility for it as canon. Where the inner presence of this subject, the Church, weakens in the souls, this process of deterioration—the breakup of the canon and the dissolution of theology as theology into a number of disciplines barely connected to each other—is inevitable. This is the great temptation of our age, in which the sense of the mystery of the Church has almost completely disappeared and the institutional Church in general is seen only as the support staff. In this view the Church can coordinate religious concerns, but does not itself enter into religion, which transpires solely in the congregation that has been deeply stirred. This is why experiencing and accepting the Church belong in the process of formation for the priesthood in a very essential way. Either "the Church awakens in the souls" during this time, or everything remains subjective in the end. Faith then becomes a private selection of what I judge to be capable of realization; the process of emptying myself and handing myself over to the words [*das Wort*] of the other does not take place. The words remain my words in the end; I do not let myself be pulled into the body of Christ but stay with my own self.

This means that because of the nature of the priesthood a comprehensive and diverse academic training is necessary. The religion of the Logos is by its very nature a rational religion. The philosophical and the historical dimensions belong to it as well as the connection to the practical; all this, however, can only be unified in relation to a truly theological core, which cannot exist without the reality "Church." It seems to me that the search for the inner unity in theology and concentration in relation to the core have become urgent priorities today in the age of growing specialization. Certainly a theologian must be broadly educated, but theology must also be able to throw the dead weight overboard again and again and to focus on what is essential. It has to be capable of distinguishing between specialized knowledge and basic knowledge. Above all it has to convey an organic view of the whole that integrates the essential concerns. If the so-called exemplary course of study leads to an accumulation of a lot of disconnected specialized knowledge, then it has missed the point. Only in the whole are the criteria also perceptible that are imperative for the badly needed discernment of spirits, for the spiritual independence of the preacher. If he does not learn to judge from the whole, he is left helplessly at the mercy of changing fashions.

This leads me to a further consideration. It has always set me thinking that in the prayer of the Roman Canon of the Mass in which the priests pray for themselves the word "sinners" appears as their designation: *nobis quoque peccatoribus*. The official self-description of clerics when facing God does not bespeak dignity; it goes to the heart of the matter. We are "sinful servants."[9] I do not think you can simply disregard this as a fake expression of humility. The same awareness is expressed here that made Isaiah call out when facing the theophany: "Woe is me! I am lost, for I am a man of unclean lips. . . ; yet my eyes have seen the King, the Lord of hosts" (Isa. 6:5). It is the same awareness that frightens Peter in the face of the miraculous catch of fish and makes him say: "Go away from me, Lord, for I am a sinful man" (Luke 5:8). It is the same awareness that echoed in the admonition of the bishop to the candidates for ordination in the old liturgy: "One must climb up to this level with great fear." It is dangerous to place yourself in the constant vicinity of the holy, which easily becomes all too familiar and ordinary and then turns into your undoing. The harsh words of Jesus to the priests and Pharisees are based on a fundamental psychological and sociological structure that always exists: habit deadens. Let us recall the example of the two students with their expedition to find the Lord's Prayer, which showed us the thirst of the pagans and our own blindness. In the past the Church was always of the opinion that you could not study theology like any other profession, simply as a means of earning money. For then we are treating the word of God like a thing that belongs to us, and this is not the case. Moses had to take off his shoes before the burning bush. We could also say that those who expose themselves to the radioactive beams of the word of God—indeed those who deal with it professionally—must be prepared to live in such a proximity or else be burned. How real this danger is can be seen by the fact that all the major crises of the Church were connected in an essential way to the clergy's downfall, for whom contact with the holy was no longer the exciting and dangerous mystery of the burning nearness of the Most Holy, but a comfortable way to make their living. The preparation that is required to be able to run the risk of professional nearness to the mystery of God can find its valid expression in the command to Moses to take off his shoes. Since shoes are made of leather, the hide of dead animals, they were regarded as a manifestation of what is dead. We must free ourselves from what is dead so that we can be in the proximity of the One who is life. The dead—these are first of all the excessive amounts of dead things, of possessions with which people surround themselves. They are also those attitudes which oppose the paschal path: only those who lose themselves find themselves. The priesthood requires leaving bourgeois existence behind; it has to incorporate the losing of oneself in a structural way. The Church's connecting celibacy and priesthood is the result of such considerations: celibacy is the strongest contradiction to the ordinary fulfillment of life. Whoever accepts the priesthood deep down inside cannot view it as a profession for making a living; rather he must somehow say yes to the renunciation of his life project and let himself be girded and led by another to a place where he really did not want to go. Before making such a decision he must hear and reflect on the words of the Lord: "For which of you, intending to build a tower, does not first sit down and estimate the cost, to see whether he has enough to complete it?" (Luke 14:28). No one can choose the priesthood for himself as his life's fulfillment. The fundamental condition is the careful consideration of whether I am complying with the call of the Lord or whether I want only my own self-fulfillment. And along the entire path there remains the condition of keeping the contact with the Lord alive. For if we turn our eyes from him we will inevitably end up like Peter on his way to Jesus across the water: only the Lord's gaze can overcome gravity—but it really can. We always remain sinners, but if his gaze holds us the waters of the deep lose their power.

In this context I would once again like to return to the *nobis quoque*, the priest's prayer in the Roman Canon. It invokes traveling companions and intercessors for the priest, to begin with John the Baptist, and, following him, two sets of seven saints: seven men, all martyrs, and seven holy women and virgins. They personify the different geographical regions of the Church and the different professions in her—the entire holy people of God,[10] The priest is dependent on the saints and on the entire living communion of the faithful for support. In my opinion it is especially meaningful that the Roman Canon mentions the names of the holy women precisely in the prayer for priests. Priestly celibacy has nothing to do with mysogyny. It does not mean the absence of a relationship to women either. The priest's inner process of maturation also depends in a very essential way on his finding the right relation to women; he needs to be supported by mothers, virgins, professional women, and widows who accept his special mission and accompany him with selfless, pure, and feminine goodness and care.

WORD AND SACRAMENT: THE PLACE OF RITUAL

We are still continuing our reflections within the framework of the idea that we should be built into a living temple. Worship—sacrifice, as the First Letter of Peter tells us—belongs to the temple. As Christians, we believe in the Word that has become flesh. For this reason priestly ministry must go beyond merely preaching and merely interpreting the Bible. What has become visible in the Word has been transformed into the sacrament, as St. Leo the Great once said.[11] The words of faith are essentially sacramental words. By its very nature, training for the priesthood must therefore be preparation for the ministry of the sacraments, for the sacramental liturgy of the Church. At this moment I do not wish to describe once again at length what this means, especially since everything I have presented thus far was already visualized in the sacramental perspective without my explicitly saying so. One thing is clear: daily celebration of the Eucharist must be the heart of all priestly formation. The chapel must form the center of the seminary, and eucharistic nearness in personal adoration before the present Lord must continue and be deepened. The sacrament of penance always has to be the live coal of purification, so to speak, as the prophet Isaiah says in the vision of his calling (Isa. 6:6–7). It has to be the power of reconciliation, which, coming from the Lord, leads us again and again from all conflict to cooperation.

Quiet is just as much a part of liturgy as festiveness. When I think back to my own years in the seminary, the moments at morning Mass with its pristine freshness and purity, along with the solemn high Masses full of celebratory splendor, are the most beautiful memories I have. Liturgy is beautiful precisely because we are not the agents but enter into something larger, which embraces us and makes us its own. I would once again like to recall the Roman Canon: In the *Communicantes* it lists the names of twenty-four saints in implicit correspondence to the twenty-four elders, who, according to the image in the Apocalypse, surround the throne of God in the heavenly liturgy.[12] Every liturgy is cosmic liturgy, a stepping out of our pathetic little groups into the towering communion that embraces heaven and earth. This gives it its reach and its great vitality. This makes each liturgy a celebration. This enriches our silence and at the same time challenges us to seek that creative obedience which enables us to sing in unison with the choir of eternity.

Cult has something to do with culture—that is evident. Culture without ritual [*Kult*] loses its soul; ritual without culture fails to recognize its own dignity. If priestly formation is liturgical formation in an essential way, at its very core, then a seminary also has to be a house of broad cultural formation. Music, literature, art, enjoying nature—all these belong here. The gifts are diverse, and the beauty of it is that the many and varied gifts can be fused into a whole in the seminary. No one can do everything, but one must not surrender to philistinism. Liturgy is the encounter with the beautiful itself, with eternal love. From it joy must radiate into the house and in it the day's tribulations can be transformed and overcome. Where liturgy becomes the center of life we are in the sphere of the words of the apostle: "Rejoice in the Lord always; again I will say, Rejoice. . . . The Lord is near" (Phil. 4:4–5). From the liturgical center, and only from here, does it become clear what Paul means when he defines the apostles, the priests of the New Covenant, as "workers . . . for your joy" (2 Cor. 1:24).

In my youth there was still occasionally the notion in rural areas that preparation for the priesthood mainly involved learning to say Mass. People wondered why this took so long, even though they knew that one also had to learn Latin to say Mass and that this was no simple matter. Rightly understood, we could indeed say that in the final analysis the preparation for the priesthood is a question of learning how to celebrate the Eucharist. But we could also turn this around and say: the Eucharist is there to teach us life. The school of the Eucharist is the school of right living; it makes us apprentices of the One who alone was entitled to say of himself: "I am the way, and the truth, and the life" (John 14:6). The frightening mandate of the Eucharist consists in the priest having permission to speak with the I of Christ. To become a priest and to be a priest mean constantly moving toward this identification. We will never accomplish this, but by seeking it we are on the right path: on the path to God and to human beings, on the path of love. All priestly formation must be measured by this standard.

NOTES

1. This was originally a lecture for the quadricentennial of the Würzburg seminary. The remark in the introduction about the purpose of anniversaries is to be understood in this context.

2. See O. Michel, "*oikos*," *Theological Dictionary of the New Testament*, 5:119–59, especially p. 130; H. A. Hoffner, "*bayith*," *Theological Dictionary of the Old Testament*, 2:107–16; M. Wodke, "*Oikos* in der Septuaginta: Erste Grundlagen," in *Hebraica*, ed. O. Rössler (Berlin, 1977), pp. 59–140, especially pp. 60ff.

3. G. Bernanos, *L'imposture* (Bibliothèque de la Pléiade, 1961), pp. 387–88.

4. Ibid., p. 352.

5. See W. Trilling, *Christusverkündigung in den synoptischen Evangelien* (Munich, 1968), p. 201; J. Gnilka, *Das Matthäusevangelium* (Freiburg, 1988), 2:476.

6. P. H. Kolvenbach, *Der österliche Weg: Exerzitien zur Lebenserneuerung* (Freiburg, 1989), p. 24.

7. H. Thielicke, *Zu Gast auf einem schönen Stern: Erinnerungen* (Hamburg, 1984), pp. 307–8.

8. See J. Ratzinger, *Schriftauslegung im Widerstreit* (Freiburg, 1989), especially pp. 7–44; on the question of the Church as the subject of theology may I refer the reader to the chapter "Theologie und Kirche" in my book *Wesen und Auftrag der Theologie* (Johannes-Verlag, 1993), pp. 39–62.

9. See J. A. Jungmann, *Missarum sollemnia* (Freiburg, 1952), 2:311 [Eng.: *The Mass of the Roman Rite* (New York, 1955), vol. 2]; Th. Schnitzler, *Die Messe in der Betrachtung* (Freiburg, 1955), 1:104–5.

10. See Th. Schnitzler, *Die Messe in der Betrachtung*, p. 105.

11. Leo the Great, "Sermo 2 de Ascensione," 2 (*PL* 54:398).

12. See Th. Schnitzler, *Die Messe in der Betrachtung* (see n. 9), p. 76; on the essence of liturgy, see J. Corbon, *Liturgie aus dem Urquell* (Einsiedeln, 1981).

Sources for the Essays

❧

1. Jesus Christ Today
   Originally published under the title "Jesus Christus Heute," *Internationale katholische Zeitschrift Communio* 19 (1990): 56–70; Spanish in *Universidad Complutense de Madrid, Jesu Cristo hoy: Curses de Verano* (El Escorial, 1989), pp. 297–316 [Eng.: *Communio: International Catholic Review* 17 (Spring, 1990): 68–87].

2. Christ and the Church: Current Problems in Theology and Consequences for Catechesis
   Originally published under the title "Christus und Kirche: Aktuelle Probleme der Theologie—Konsequenzen für die Katechese," in Ratzinger, Staudinger, and Schütte, *Zu Grundfragen der Theologie heute* (Paderborn, 1992), pp. 7–17.

3. God's Power—Our Hope
   Originally published under the title "Gottes Macht—Unsere Hoffnung," *Pastoralblatt für die Diözesen Aachen, Berlin, Essen, Hildesheim, Köln, Osnabrück* 40 (1988): 71–83.

4. The Resurrection as the Foundation of Christian Liturgy: On the Meaning of Sunday for Christian Prayer and Christian Life
   Originally published under the title "Vom Sinn des Sonntags," *Forum katholischer Theologie* 1 (1985): 161–75, as well as in different language editions of *Communio: International Catholic Review*.

5. "Built from Living Stones": The House of God and the Christian Way of Worshiping God
Originally published under the title "'Auferbaut aus lebendigen Steinen': Das Gotteshaus und die christliche Weise der Gottesverehrung," in *Kirche aus lebendigen Steinen,* ed. W. Seidel (Mainz, 1975), pp. 30–48.

6. "Sing Artistically for God": Biblical Directives for Church Music
Originally published under the title "Biblische Vorgaben für die Kirchenmusik," in *Brixener Initiative Musik und Kirche: Drittes Symposion "Choral und Mehrstimmigkeit"* (Brixen, 1990), pp. 9–21.

7. The Image of the World and of Human Beings in the Liturgy and Its Expression in Church Music
Originally published under the title "Liturgie und Kirchenmusik," *Internationale katholische Zeitschrift Communio* 15 (1986): 243–56, as well as in *Musices aptatio, Jahrbuch 1986: Christus in Ecclesia cantat,* German edition (Rome, 1986): 60–74 and in the English, Italian, French and Portuguese editions of this volume (Rome, 1986).

8. "In the Presence of the Angels I Will Sing Your Praise": The Regensburg Tradition and the Reform of the Liturgy
Originally published under the title "In der Spannung zwischen Regensburger Tradition und nachkonziliarar Reform," *Musica sacra: Zeitschrift des Allgemeinen Cäcilienverbandes für Deutschland* 114 (1994): 379–89.

9. A Discussion between F. Greiner and J. Ratzinger
Originally published under the title "Kirchenverfassung und Umkehr," *Internationale katholische Zeitschrift Communio* 13 (1984): 444–57 (considerably abridged here).

10. Preparation for Priestly Ministry
Originally published under the title "Perspektiven der Priesterausbildung heute," in *Unser Auftrag: Besinnung auf den priesterlichen Dienst,* ed. K. Hillenbrand (Würzburg, 1990), pp. 11–38.